MORALITY
AND THE
MARKET PLACE

London Lectures in Contemporary Christianity 1980

Brian Griffiths

Hodder & Stoughton

LONDON SYDNEY AUCKLAND TORONTO

TO RACHEL

British Library Cataloguing in Publication Data

Griffiths, Brian, 1941–
  Morality and the market place.
  1. Christianity and politics
  I. Title
  261.7   BR115.P7

ISBN 0 340 26354 7

CONTENTS

ACKNOWLEDGMENTS

This book is based on a series of lectures — the London Lectures in Contemporary Christianity — which I gave at St Andrew Undershaft in the City of London in the spring of 1980, and then at the Brookings Institution in Washington, DC, in the summer of that year. I am deeply grateful to the Trustees of the Lectures for inviting me to deliver the 1980 series and also to the C.S. Lewis Institute in Washington for sponsoring them in the United States. I would like to express my thanks to the late Lord Armstrong, Lord Robbins, the Reverend Prebendary Dick Lucas, William Deedes and Lord Caldecote who acted as chairmen for the lectures in London and to Bruce Maclaury, Lawrence Krause, Bob Hamrin and Marvin Kosters who acted as chairmen in Washington. I owe a special debt to the Reverend Doctor John Stott for his constant encouragement and criticism of the subject matter and above all for his desire that a Christian mind be brought to bear on the subject of the lectures. I am also grateful to Douglas Evans for reading the first two chapters and to my secretary Agatha Bobb for typing the manuscript and coping so calmly with unreasonable demands at short notice.

Last and most of all, I owe an enormous debt to my wife and children for putting up with my absence from family life to prepare and deliver the lectures. I owe a particular thanks to my wife Rachel, who more than anyone else has discussed these issues with me over the years, who read the manuscript and made numerous suggestions on both content and style.

Muswell Hill
December 1981

PREFACE

This book is the text of a series of lectures which I gave in the spring of 1980. The lectures were a response to a challenge posed some years earlier by Milton Friedman. 'How can you be a Christian,' he said, 'and advocate the market economy? After all didn't Jesus say that it is more difficult for a camel to pass through the eye of a needle than for a rich man to enter the Kingdom of Heaven?'

This question proved a turning point for me. Throughout my time as a student at the London School of Economics, I had found socialism attractive because of its professed belief in justice and its concern for the disadvantaged. As the sixties progressed, the practice of socialism proved to be very different from its rhetoric. The economy was in a constant state of crisis, the trade unions grew more powerful and destructive, while strikes and protests exposed deep and growing conflict within society, against which the appeal to a social contract seemed hollow. Eventually the government was forced to hand over control of our economy to the International Monetary Fund. It also became clear that modern socialism was being driven by two major forces, Marxism and secularism, both of which were deeply unattractive, and ultimately antagonistic, to those who professed the Christian faith.

Over these years, I studied and then taught economics. I soon found that the case for free enterprise and free markets and against public ownership and control was overwhelming. Markets worked — they literally delivered the goods. Yet I was always uneasy with using the expression 'capitalism' as a way of describing the market economy. The 'ism' of capitalism was too closely linked historically to the 'survival of the fittest'; and more recently it had become too identified with the view that literally everything should be bought and sold. Such an 'ism' in which the individual is treated as autonomous, and choice as sovereign, fits uneasily into a Christian view of the world. In addition, at this time capitalism itself was charged with being in a state of crisis, partly because of global inflation and partly because of the perception that economic growth involved high costs especially in relation to the environment.

It was then that Friedman posed his question.

The reason for reprinting the lectures is that his question remains a valid one. So, hopefully, does the response. The argument of the lectures is that the long term problem, with both libertarian capitalism and socialism, is their neglect, or worse still, their rejection of any religious basis for life. If either individual freedom or government control become *the* driving force of a society, the problem arises of how to limit these forces. It is a problem which results from the growth of secular humanism over the last two centuries. I have come to believe that it is a problem which is insoluble without appealing to a moral standard which ultimately derives from a religious foundation.

The tragedy of the modern world is that religion has been relegated to the private domain, and appears irrelevant to the major themes of public policy. Historically neither Judaism nor Christianity ever conceived of themselves as restricted to private matters. Both the Old and New Testaments have a great deal to say about economic and political life. They are not just confined to matters of personal integrity and good behaviour, but have a bearing on the institutional arrangements of our society and the goals which governments pursue. The parable of the talents, to take one example, is about the productive use of resources, whether private or public.

On the basis of biblical evidence, I continue to advocate the seven guidelines which I proposed as of contemporary importance: they are, the legitimacy of wealth creation, the necessity of private property rather than state ownership, as the norm for ownership the ability of each family to retain a permanent stake in the economy, the mandate on the community to relieve poverty rather than pursue equality, the requirement for government to remedy injustice, the caution against materialism and the importance of accountability and judgement in the whole of life. These mean that a Christian perspective is distinct from either secular capitalism or Marxism. If asked to describe such a world, I would characterise it as a market economy bounded by biblical principles of justice. It is this idea which the lectures sought to champion.

Since the lectures were given there have been considerable changes in this country — the success of government policies aimed at wealth creation, the spread of privatisation and the way in which it has been copied by other countries, the acknowledgement by Soviet leadership of the weaknesses of their own state centred system, the introduction of choice in education, housing and health, new ways of dealing with the problems of inner cities. These and numerous other points would need to be included if the lectures were to be given today. But, three major points should be emphasised.

One is the issue of theological method. This is an area which needs elaboration. I devoted only one lecture to it, whereas it deserves a series of lectures in its own right. Most people who advocate socialist policies and who attempt to underpin them theologically, do so by using a social gospel based on either the theology of the Kingdom of God or liberation theology. I have serious reservations with the way both of these deal with the biblical text itself. Instead of allowing the text to speak for itself, liberation theology accepts uncritically an economic and political ideology based on Marxism and then interprets the text within this framework. It confuses material with spiritual poverty and refuses to take seriously original sin and human selfishness. As a result, its interpretation of the Exodus as a political event and its understanding of salvation in terms of changed political

9

structures, fails to do justice to either the Pentateuch or Christ's teaching on the nature of salvation and freedom.

More significant in this country than liberation theologians are those who make the Kingdom of God synonymous with a rather vague concept of a sharing and caring community, which, when linked to the Incarnation, drifts into a political programme of equality, at the expense of individual freedom, and large government spending, at the expense of wealth creation. Many contemporary church people find their inspiration for this view in their understanding of the Kingdom of God. Yet, as John Stott argues, the Kingdom of God in the gospels is at heart a Christological concept, so that it may be said to exist only where Jesus is consciously acknowledged as Lord.

Hence the Kingdom is relevant to personal ethics. It is also the basis for the life of the Church. But it contains little of practical significance for the public policy issues raised by politics and economics. In so much modern writing, clear biblical words such as 'love', 'the poor' and 'sharing' are removed from their immediate context to become slogans for wealth redistribution. The pursuit of greater social and economic equality is identified as the necessary expression of equality in the sight of God. While our responsibility to others is at the heart of Jesus' teaching, it is quite wrong to make it synonymous with equality.

By contrast, the theology of social ethics which underlies the lectures is one based on creation ethics — the search for those universal moral principles and structures which are part of the creation order and which are expanded on in Old Testament law. Despite the exegetical problems in relating the Old Testament to the modern world, there is a wealth of material which relates social structures (marriage, ownership, family, law etc) to the moral law (the Ten Commandments etc). This again is an area which needs greater elaboration.

A second issue and something which is not touched on in the book but which I have subsequently come to see as important is what Peter Berger and Richard Neuhaus termed 'mediating structures' or what Edmund Burke chose to call 'the little platoons' of our society. They are all those institutions — the family, the school, the workplace, the village, the neighbourhood, the trade union, the professional association, the church — which allow people to pursue particular interests and to participate in the life of different communities. They *mediate* between the private life of the individual and the great megastructures of our society. Burke saw them as not just helping people in their private lives but as fulfilling a political function. 'To be attached to the subdivision, to love the little platoon we belong to in society, is the first principle (the germ as it were) of public affections. It is the first link in the series by which we proceed towards a love of our country, and of mankind.' Because a healthy democracy will consist of robust mediating structures, public policy needs to protect and foster such structures, and wherever possible, use such structures in the pursuit of social policy. It is no accident that traditional Marxism has been committed to destroying mediating structures by bringing them within the orbit of the state.

Throughout this book, and this is the third issue which needs to be emphasised, the place of values has been central to the case we have been trying to make. Whether in the family, the school, the workplace or the community, the values which people espouse and which guide their lives, are important to our economic and political life. Mediating structures help generate and maintain values. In the battle against crime and hooliganism, in appealing for responsible stewardship of the environment, in helping prevent drug abuse and homelessness, the need for permanent values to be transmitted from one generation to the next through the family and through schools, is important. Government can achieve a certain amount through legislation and persuasion. But that is, of necessity, limited.

Even those who remain agnostic about personal belief recognise that the continued existence of the market economy and democratic institutions depends on the widespread acceptance of certain values. However, as a result of the growing influence of Marx and Freud, the acceptance of these traditional values can no longer be taken for granted.

More than any other mediating structure, the Church has been, and should be, the most important source of values in our society. The tragedy in Britain today is that the institutional Churches — save for some exceptions, such as the Black Churches — are in decline. The decline of the Church is a nettle which only the Church itself can grasp. If it does not, the consequences are enormous. The good news, however, is that it can grasp the nettle. It has done so in the past. And it can do so again. Were these lectures to be given again, an elaboration of the part it should play in our society would be an important final chapter.

BRIAN GRIFFITHS
London   February 1989

CHAPTER 1
THE CRISIS OF CAPITALISM

By profession I am both a Christian and an economist. Yet we live in a society in which there are very great pressures on us to keep those subjects in watertight compartments. For many people Christianity represents values; economic facts. Propositions relating to Christianity are normative; propositions relating to economics are positive. One of my lasting impressions as an undergraduate studying at the London School of Economics in the early 1960s, dominated as it was by the Popperian conception of science and the quest for a Positive Economics, was of the great gulf that was fixed between the two worlds of social science and religious belief. Yet I always questioned whether this separation was not more apparent than real. I was curious that the branch of economics which related to the welfare of individuals and societies, namely welfare economics, depended on an explicit set of judgments, which seemed remarkably similar to contemporary liberal values. And I was even more curious as to why it was that Milton Friedman could so confidently assert in his writings a belief in the value of freedom, or Harry Johnson in the value of efficiency or Nicholas Kaldor in the value of equality, if it were true that facts and values could be distinguished so clearly.

What has frankly surprised me about the last decade is the way in which social scientists who make no claim to a Christian profession have been talking openly about the relevance of religious values to our current economic problems in the Western world. Let me give you some examples:

In *Social Limits to Growth,* the late Fred Hirsch wrote:

Truth, trust, acceptance, restraint, obligation — these are among the social virtues grounded in religious belief which are also now seen to play a central role in the functioning of an individualistic, contractual economy. To this extent, the pay-off to religious belief is in earthy coin. The traditional concept of religion as insurance on the next world which might or not pay off in this one is exactly reversed.[1]

One of the leading neo-Conservative commentators in the United States, Irving Kristol in 'The Disaffection from Capitalism and Socialism' states that:

Capitalism survives because it still satisfies the basic, simple impulses of ordinary men and women. It will not continue to satisfy them however, without the bedrock provided by the Judeo–Christian tradition that ordinary men and women need — that we all need. It gives certain answers to ultimate questions that modern philosophy or modern thought of whatever kind cannot provide . . . to the degree that organised religion has decayed and the attachment to the Judeo–Christian tradition has become weaker, to that degree capitalism has become uglier and less justifiable.[2]

And the distinguished British economist, Ezra J. Mishan, writing of the disillusion with economic growth in The *Economic Growth Debate* puts it that:

Modern economic growth, and the norms and attitudes it establishes, have produced a highly complex industrial and urban organisation, albeit one that is increasingly vulnerable largely because the spread of affluence, and the sheer rapidity of change, have combined, unavoidably to undermine the complex of institutions and myths that invested all pre-industrial civilisations with stability and cohesion. The existing libertarian order in the West is no longer rooted in a consensus that drains its inspiration ultimately from a common set of unquestioned beliefs. The legitimacy of all its institutions are perpetually under assault. Social order is visibly disintegrating.[3]

14

It is against this background that I wish to consider the contemporary Crisis of Capitalism. Before we do so however it is important to be clear about the meaning of certain terms. A pure capitalist economic system would be one in which property was privately owned, so that all goods and services would be produced by private enterprise in response to economic incentives. The involvement of the government in economic life would be minimal, concerned primarily with running the legal system and conceivably the military and the police. A pure socialist economic system, by contrast, would be one in which all property was publicly owned so that all goods and services would be produced by state enterprises and in response to political priorities. Any use of markets would be limited and controlled by government. In reality of course there is never a pure economic system of the kind just described. However, the difference between the systems of property rights in countries such as Britain, America, Germany, Hong Kong and Indonesia on the one hand and Russia, East Germany, Vietnam and China, is still sufficiently great to enable us to label the former capitalist and the latter socialist.

The record of capitalism over the past 200 years in transforming the standard of living of the Western world is remarkable. In England during the period between the end of the eighteenth century and the beginning of the Second World War there was an increase in goods and services per person of four- to six-fold at a time when population was increasing six-fold. The rise in total goods and services available over this period is put at between thirty-fold and fifty-fold. Throughout the nineteenth century output per person grew at a rate of 1.5 per cent per annum. As a result of the introduction of machines and the growth of markets, relatively unrestricted by government, the standard of living for the average British person — judged in terms of food, clothing, shelter, health, life expectancy, infant mortality, education and material possessions — increased on an unprecedented scale over these years. By 1900

15

the kind of poverty, famine and illiteracy which is still prevalent in many parts of the globe had been removed.[4] Alongside the increasing prosperity was a widespread belief that the system of free enterprise which had produced this was not only efficient but just. Although people were endowed with different abilities and suffered varying degrees of misfortune, capitalism held out the promise that hard work and frugality would lead to increased prosperity for all those who wished to avail themselves of the opportunities it offered.

One does not have to be a Marxist to observe that by comparison something seems to have gone badly wrong in the capitalist societies of the Western world over the last two decades. To begin with there is the question of performance. One thing of which capitalism has always been proud, is that it can in a literal sense 'deliver the goods'. However, since the late 1960s — roughly speaking from the time of the escalation of the Vietnam War and the student riots in Paris — the rate of growth of gross national product in real terms in all Western countries has fallen noticeably. At the same time unemployment has risen to new levels for the post-war years and continues to remain high. But more disturbing that either of these has been an increase in the rate of inflation which has affected all countries and which continues to remain high in many. A high and uncertain rate of inflation is disturbing because it reduces the efficiency of the market economy and slows down the process of economic growth. Inflation encourages consumption, borrowing and speculation: it discourages saving, lending and investment. The investment which takes place is in hedges against inflation rather than productive industries. If governments respond, as they typically do by intervention to control price and wage rises, the inefficiency created by inflation is only compounded.

More serious over the longer run is whether capitalist economies can survive a period of sustained inflation. In his classic monetarist analysis of inflation published just after the end of the First World War, J.M. Keynes wrote:

16

Lenin is said to have declared that the best way to destroy the capitalism system was to debauch the currency . . . Lenin was certainly right. There is no subtler, no surer way of overturning the existing basis of society than to debauch the currency. The process engages all the hidden forces of economic law on the side of destruction and it does it in a manner which not one man in a million is able to diagnose.[5]

Already we can see this process at work. The most damaging effect of inflation on society is the capricious redistribution of income and wealth which it produces. As the outcome bears no relation to either an efficient market or the declared aims of government policy, it sets up pressures for those who feel injured to seek political solutions, which mean greater government intervention and greater inefficiency — a treadmill with which I regret to say we are all too familiar in the United Kingdom.

Doubts about the ability of the system to survive arise in another context, namely that of ecology and pollution. Even if inflation can be contained, there remains the question of whether a lower rate of economic growth in the Western world can be sustained in view of the demands which it makes on the limited resources of our planet, especially food and minerals. The pessimistic report presented to the Club of Rome in 1972, 'The Limits to Growth', received much publicity on this issue; yet the results of many other studies on this subject are equally pessimistic.[6] They suggest that if current trends in world population growth, industrialisation, pollution, food production and the depletion of non-renewable resources continues, then within a short space of time, perhaps less than a hundred years, economic growth will come to a halt, the industrial base of the world economy will collapse and finally after severe global recession and famine, not only will population growth fall dramatically but so will the level of population itself.

Although I have serious reservations about the methodology of most of these studies (in that they are far too pessimistic

17

about the ability of the business community to respond to changing circumstances following changing relative prices) and although some of the shortages which appear are due not so much to the limits of nature as the intervention and regulation of governments, nevertheless they raise sufficiently serious doubts about such things as the effects of carbon dioxide and the present lack of adequate recycling that I believe they must be taken seriously. In any event, they are being taken sufficiently seriously by a large number of people to raise strong doubts in the minds of many about the viability of our present system.

Even if continued economic growth proved feasible there remains the question of whether it is desirable. The desirability of continued economic growth has been raised by a number of economists over the past decade and the titles of their publications make their conclusions clear — *Does Money Buy Happiness?* (Easterlin),[7] *The Joyless Economy* (Scitovsky),[8] *The Costs of Economic Growth* (Mishan).[9]

Traditional economic analysis is premised on the assumption that more is better. Yet it is this very assumption which these writers call into question. Their starting point is the observation that despite periods of sustained economic growth and increasing prosperity all social statistics indicate a growing sense of malaise and unfulfilment. Pollution of the air, ocean and soil continues unabated. Cities which were once beautiful have been rendered ugly. Atmospheric pollution continues to rise. Indicators of social disintegration such as divorce, suicide, delinquency, petty theft, drug taking, sexual deviance, crime and violence all show an ever-increasing upward movement. The conclusion which is reached is quite startling. Professor Mishan argues that 'it is now reasonable to believe that, despite the abundance of man-made goods produced by continued growth, its net effect on human health and happiness could be adverse and possible disastrous'.[10] If true this undermines any claim to efficiency made for the market economy.

In addition to doubts over the ability of the system to survive, there is a noticeable loss of confidence in the basic institutions of the system itself: corporations, trade unions and governments. The most distinctive institution of capitalist economies is the privately owned corporation. Yet it is this, and in particular the multi-national corporation, which has become the object of bitter criticism. Large corporations are accused of exercising both economic and political power for their own rather than the public interest, of exploiting their workers, polluting the environment and stripping the world of its natural resources. Multinational companies are viewed as beyond the control of any single government, intent on maximising their global profits without regard to the needs and interests of individual countries. Similarly, trade unions are thought of as institutions whose objectives and practices are fundamentally opposed to the public interest. By using their monopoly power (which in the case of the UK is protected by law) they are able to increase their relative wages, veto industrial change and disrupt production for purely political reasons. At the same time as there is growing disaffection with large corporations and trade unions there is also a loss of confidence in government to take the necessary action to redress the balance. In the case of trade union reform in the UK this is partly because government has tried and failed but more generally because the public sector is now viewed as having a self-interest which need bear no relation to the public interest.

The loss of confidence in the basic economic institutions of Western societies is based on the view that the results of the system bear little relation to certain norms of justice. Such a loss of confidence is not confined to the developed countries of the Western world. It has a global dimension. In the Third World the charge is that the present international economic order is funamentally unjust, with a minority of the world's population consuming an enormous share of the world's GNP, not to mention their extravagant consumption of a limited amount of non-renewable resources. On the assumption that the economic inequality between the North and the South, the 'haves' and the 'have-nots', cannot be allowed to continue, capitalism comes under attack as the engine providing the force to sustain such inequality. If inequality is to be reduced, so the argument goes,

19

capitalism must be either abandoned or at the very least changed radically.

In the light, therefore, of the deteriorating performance of capitalist economies and the chorus of criticism which has emerged of the market economy, it is difficult to avoid the conclusion that something important has begun to go wrong with capitalism as we now know it. In my judgment the present crisis is above all a crisis regarding the legitimacy of the system itself. For any economic system to work and survive it must be considered legitimate. People must have confidence in it. *First* they must have confidence that it will work: that it can produce the kinds of things which they want to buy. If there are no goods in the shops; or if food can only be obtained by rationing; or if the state siphons off the lion's share of increased earnings as taxation; or if an economy seems incapable of growing, then people begin to question the fundamentals on which such a system is built.

Second, it must be considered just. No one expects an economic system to produce absolute justice. This is no quest for some Utopia. But people do expect that the rewards which are sought and gained in economic life bear some relationship to traditionally accepted standards of justice. It would be difficult to justify an economic system in which wages were determined by a form of lottery; or in which monopoly and exploitation were the order of day; or, in which each person earned the same wage regardless of effort, risk or training. Why? Because these would offend canons of justice which find acceptance among a large proportion of the population.

Third, the system must be capable of survival. If on the basis of the best information the system is seen to be heading for some sort of catastrophe then people not unnaturally lose confidence in it.

It is precisely this sense of legitimacy which is lacking in capitalist societies today. Inflation has undermined the legitimacy of the market order. The oil crisis has brought into focus the legitimacy of the West consuming such a large proportion of such an important non-renewable resource. The closed shop and the wildcat strike have undermined the legitimacy of modern trade unionism. Low wages and large bribes have questioned the legitimacy of the multi-nationals. And growing government, increasing bureaucracy, higher taxes and more and more regulation have put the legitimacy of government itself at issue.

Explaining the Crisis

Attempts to explain the 'crisis' are many and various. Nevertheless it is possible to distinguish a number of broadly different approaches and we shall consider four.

1. *The Marxist*

With this approach the current crisis of Western societies is the inevitable outcome of the contradictions implicit in capitalism society, all of which derive ultimately from the ownership of the means of production being in private hands. For the Marxist, history is a process in which society is transformed from a primitive state through slavery, feudalism, capitalism, socialism and finally communism. Change takes place because of social conflict and in each stage except the last, conflict is the result of the exploitation of the majority by the minority based on the ownership of property and the consequent manipulation of culture. The crisis of capitalism therefore is the crisis of a society based on the exploitation of the labour force through the pursuit of private profit, the exploitation of women through the bourgeois family and the exploitation of colonial peoples through the abuse of minorities and the rise of neo-colonialism in the form of multi-national corporations and US foreign policy. In a Marxist world-view the inevitability of socialism results from the failures of capitalism.

2. *Schumpeter*

A similar yet separate approach which foresaw the demise of

capitalism and the growth of socialism, without necessarily however postulating the inevitability of a crisis, was that developed by Schumpeter.[11] His approach was different from Marx's in that it was not a prediction of the future based on inexorable laws in history, but a probable result based on 'observable tendencies'. Although he wrote just after the Great Depression of the nineteen-thirties, he rejected the idea that capitalism would break down because of a lack of investment opportunities and a reduction in the real rate of profit. The problem with capitalism was not that it would fail, but that it would continue its remarkable success in raising real output and real consumption per capita, which in turn would have the effects of undermining those very social institutions on which its success depended, and creating a civilisation hostile to its continued existence.

Schumpeter developed a number of avenues to show how this might come about. In the *first* place, the entrepreneurial function was likely to become redundant, largely because innovation would be taken over by teams of specialists in large corporations. *Next,* the process of expansion would undermine all those institutions which expressed the highly personalised private enterprise which for him was the essence of capitalism (such as the change in ownership from individual proprietorship to equity participation in large corporations), as well as destroy the protecting strata — the aristocracy, farmers and small business — on which it depended. *Third,* it would foster a rational spirit and criticism which would turn in on itself and which is highlighted by a class of intellectuals who, according to Schumpeter, have 'a vested interest in social unrest'. In Schumpeter's scheme therefore the self-destruction of capitalism as a system is inherent in its success. Although not a Marxist, Schumpeter's analysis of the ability of capitalism to survive had a number of common characteristics shared by the Marxists. To start with, his answer to the question, 'Can capitalism survive?' was a resounding no, while his answer to the question 'Can socialism work?' was a resounding yes. In his scheme economic factors are the prime mover of change. Not

22

only that but the decline of capitalism was of such a character each step taken represented a positive move in the direction of socialism.

3. *Technology*

An equally deterministic yet non-Marxist approach to explaining the crisis can be found in the writings of Galbraith,[12] Mishan[13] and Ellul.[14] Here the emphasis is on technology as an autonomous and primary force driving our society in a certain direction. By technology is meant the systematic application of scientific knowledge to practical tasks. Complex technology requires large-scale production, and so the need for huge investments of capital and large organisational structures. The major factor leading to the growth of large business units is therefore modern technology. Technology is indifferent to ideology; the same trends are visible in large private corporations in the US and in state enterprises in the USSR. In Galbraith's view technology is producing a convergence of the two rival systems — capitalism and socialism. Because capitalism is the servant of technology, and technology dictates the scale of modern life, so capitalism is being inexorably transformed into an economy of planning. Galbraith's analysis of American industry in *The New Industrial State* is that of a planned economy — the only difference between it and the USSR being that the planning decision of the 200 largest US corporations are uncoordinated. In this view, therefore, the 'crisis' facing capitalism is the result of an independent technology driving it in a direction which runs counter to the declared ideology of the technostructure who control it.

Others such as Jacques Ellul and E.J. Mishan see a far more sinister side to technology. Technological innovation is the source of many manufacturing processes which produce harmful pollutants, of products which cause great harm in themselves and of processes which permit immense powers of control by governments over individuals. Technology has made possible contemporary forms of violence, terrorism and urban

23

disruption. Worst of all are the perils of nuclear energy whether used for peace or war. One of the consequences of the increasing hazards presented by new technology therefore is the demand for greater government intervention.

In *The Technological Society,* Jacques Ellul emphasises the dehumanising elements of technology. He claims that the problem is not just one of machines but also of technique with its emphasis on rationality and efficiency being applied in every field of human activity. Having stormed the world it has entered, it has now permeated the whole of our lives. 'But when technique enters into every area of life, including the human, it ceases to be external to man and becomes his very substance. It is no longer face to face with him but is integrated with him and it progressively absorbs him. In this respect technique is radically different from the machine. This transformation, so obvious in modern society is the result of the fact that technique has become autonomous.'[15] One particularly adverse effect of technique is in work. Because under a capitalist system work is concerned with optimising and efficiency, 'the important concern is not the psychic and mental structure of the human being but the interrupted flow of any and all goods which invention allows the economy to produce'.

4. *Government*

For many who adopt a liberal and free-enterprise approach the explanation of our present problems is the increasing role which government has come to play in our economic life. Whichever indicator one cares to use of the role of the government in economic life — government expenditure as a percentage of GNP, total tax revenue relative to income, the range of activities in which the government is involved as producer, the extent to which economic life is subject to some form or other of regulation — all show a similar long-term growth in periods of peacetime throughout the present century. The twentieth century is a period during which economic life has become increasingly politicised. Areas of the economy in which formerly goods and services such as medicine, education, transport and energy were supplied by the private sector, have been taken over by the public sector and the key issues as to how much should be supplied and at what price, have been decided directly or indirectly by the ballot box rather than the market place.

From this perspective the problem is that governments have interfered increasingly with the workings of the market economy and reduced its efficiency. The heart of the problem has been governments' concern with social justice and an egalitarian distribution of income which has led them into passing legislation which has increased the costs of doing business. At the same time by increasing their expenditure programmes at a rate far greater than the growth in tax revenue they have been led into creating inflation.

As the ballot box rather than the market place has been used to decide the allocation of resources, so the power of the individual has diminished and the power of the corporate state — which effects some form of social contract between corporations, trade unions and government — increased. The critical question is whether this trend is reversible. Various democratic governments have been elected with a mandate to reduce the size of government. But in no Western country so far, other than in the years following the end of a war, has there been a major permanent reduction in the role of the state.

A number of the explanations of the crisis which we have examined seem to contain an element of truth. Schumpeter had considerable insight in his analysis of the contradictions implicit in capitalism which produced the change from an entrepreneurial to a bureaucratic style. The complexity of modern technology has had an important influence on the scale of life in modern society. Few would doubt that the rise of government has produced economic inefficiency and restricted the freedom of choice. But by themselves each of these explanations is partial. More important is the fact that none of them can be divorced from the realm of values. To the extent that people are prepared to accept that there is a crisis of capitalism there is a great tendency to see the problem as comparable to a machine breaking down; either there is not enough oil, or else a part needs to be replaced or else some bolt needs to be tightened. In other words, it is to argue that the problem is a *technical* problem which admits of a *technical* solution. If central banks printed less money, inflation would be controlled; if property rights were more clearly defined, pollution would diminish; if taxation was reduced the rate of growth of output would rise. I happen to agree with all of these propositions. But I am more and more convinced that the problem is not at heart a *technical* problem capable of a technical solution but a moral problem concerned with the values of our age. We cannot consider the growth of technology or the growth of government as autonomous forces which are somehow independent of the set of values which have either accompanied or prompted their growth. Similarly, it is because of the prevailing values of our society that it is so difficult to implement what at least to economists appear to be technically feasible solutions to our problems.

The Real Crisis — the Crisis of Humanism

I would like to develop a particular thesis to explain the contemporary crisis of capitalism which incorporates certain of the insights derived from all these approaches but which is anchored in a Christian world-view. In doing so I should like to express my gratitude to the late Herman Dooyeweerd and to Irving Kristol both of whom have influenced my thinking.[16]

In order to develop my theme I need to make three important assumptions. The first is that to understand any society it is necessary to consider the religious basis of that society. Religion plays a vital role in society because it provides an explanation of origin and destiny, of identity and purpose. By declaring a set of absolutes, it supplies standards as well as goals for both individuals and institutions. By providing an intellectual framework through which people interpret reality and understand

26

history it must of necessity shape our culture. As a result the science, education, art, technology and institutions of a society are dependent on its religious motive. Religion therefore is more than just a personal affair and its influence in society is more than the sum of its influences on individuals. By moulding the prevailing climate of opinion it influences values which in turn both influence events and fashion institutions.

Next I would wish to assert the truth of the Christian revelation. Although I do not wish to dwell on it at this stage I feel I should say something regarding my understanding of Christianity. Above everything else the Christian religion claims to be a revealed religion. God is revealed in nature, in his Word but most of all in his Incarnate Son. He is revealed as the creator of this world and we, made in his image, are appointed as trustees over the physical universe. By declaring independence from God man fell and the fall of man has had cataclysmic effects, which permeate every facet of our lives and our culture. But because of his love for us, in the person of Jesus Christ, redemption is made possible for us all. The relevance of Pentecost is that through the person of the Holy Spirit these propositions can acquire a personal dimension which in turn should influence our thinking and our behaviour. The real importance of the Christian religion is that it claims to be true irrespective of how I regard it.

This brings me to my third assumption. Asserting the truth of the Christian revelation has one very important implication. If Christianity is true and if religion affects culture, then non-Christian religions, whose creeds must at some point involve the denial of some aspect of Christian truth, will reveal cultural problems resulting from inconsistencies which are impossible to reconcile given their religious postulates.

The relevance of this can be seen by considering the present religious force in Western culture, namely a humanism which finds its embodiment in liberalism. Ever since the Renaissance, but particularly since the Enlightenment of the eighteenth century, Western culture has become imbued with a humanistic and a libertarian spirit. As a religion humanism affirms some important absolutes. It starts by proclaiming that God is dead or what comes to the same thing, that if he exists he is irrelevant. From this it follows that 'man is the measure of all things'. Man is free and autonomous. He ·is independent of all authority except that of his own choosing. He is free to choose anything and everything. In no area of life is choice restricted. Because of this faith in the perfectibility of man, liberalism fostered a great belief in progress — history was seen as the emancipation of mankind from ignorance, taboos, constraints, crime and war through the process of education and increasing material prosperity. Economic growth as an objective of national economic policy was a natural part therefore of a liberal view of the world. Alongside the emphasis on knowledge, great faith was also placed in the power of science to discover the laws of the physical universe, society and even human personality itself, so that the world and individuals could be improved by being controlled.

It is important to notice that liberalism in the sense in which I have just defined it is at the root of both socialism and capitalism as economic ideologies. It is no accident that the intellectual defence of modern capitalism and the major contemporary expression of socialism, namely Marxism, both depend on the assumptions of the Enlightenment and date from that period. The difference between the two is a debate over means but the end — namely freedom — remains the same.

The major point I wish to make in this chapter can now be stated. Liberalism has always had a tension between science and freedom: the imperative to control and the free expression of the human personality. Capitalism has attempted to construct and defend an economic system which embodies both but in which freedom is ultimately more important than control. Control is exercised within the corporation, the trade union and the government. Freedom is exercised in the market. By contrast socialism reverses the priorities: control is more important than freedom; and control extends to the whole of the economy, with concessions to freedom being minimal. But because both systems deify one aspect of reality they produce problems which are insoluble within their own terms of reference. I believe this is precisely what the 'crisis of capitalism' is about. It is nothing less than the crisis of humanism as a religion being played out in economic life. If freedom is made an absolute, as it is for example in the writings of Milton Friedman and Friedrich Hayek, such that it is impossible on intellectual grounds to place limits on the exercise of freedom, the result is an economic system shorn of justice. I have never met anyone who objected to capitalism because it relied on the freedom of the individual to buy and sell, to produce and innovate, to save and invest. But I have met many who objected to the kind of society it has created because of its injustice and inhumanity. My contention is that both the justice and inhumanity of capitalist societies result inevitably from the failure to assert certain absolutes and so place proper limits on the use of freedom.

The Hayekian Defence of the Market Place

This is a thesis which runs quite counter to Milton and Rose Friedman's latest book, *Free to Choose,* the basic theme of which is that our problems today result from the intervention of government.[17] To help us in understanding this basic theme I have chosen to examine Professor Hayek's monumental defence of the market economy, *Law, Legislation and Liberty.*[18] I do so because he mades much clearer the philosophical basis of such a position than Milton Friedman does in, for example, *Capitalism and Freedom.* It is rooted in his own quite complex philosophy but if we really wish to understand his argument we must start at a rather abstract level.

Hayek suggests that there are two ways of looking at human activities and institutions. One is to conceive of them as being deliberately designed for the purposes they serve, the implication of which is that we should be constantly reforming existing institutions so that they may better serve those ends for which they were intended. The point here is that institutions are useful only if they have been designed to achieve a particular

29

purpose. The other view is that institutions have just evolved. The evolutionary view is that the only explanation for certain practices being adopted and others discarded, is that these practices enable the group which adopts them to survive and gain mastery over others. To Hayek the foundation of social theory is that there are orderly structures in existence which, although the result of the action of many people, do not result from any particular human design. In the physical world examples of such spontaneous orders are the growth of crystals or complex organic compounds and in the social world the growth of language, law, money and morals. Although there was a time says Hayek 'when men believed that even language and morals had been "invented" by some genius of the past, everybody recognises now that they are the outcome of a process of evolution whose results nobody foresaw or designed'.[19]

The use of an evolutionary approach such as this in explaining these phenomena is itself not new. It was developed in the eighteenth century by writers like Hume, Mandeville and Smith and applied by Darwin in the field of biology in the nineteenth century. Incidentally, in this area, it is Darwin who is derivative of the moral philosophers and not as is commonly supposed, largely I think because of the work of Spencer, the other way around.

For Hayek, the growth of the market economy can be explained only in this evolutionary framework. It is another example of a spontaneous order. Nobody invented it. It just grew up. In the context of a market, however, the use of economy is a misleading term. Used strictly whether in reference to a household, a corporation or a government, an economy consists of a set of activities by which scarce means are allocated to specific ends. But in the market order there is no such hierarchy of ends. 'It serves the multiplicity of separate and incommensurable ends of all its separate members.' Because of the confusion which might result from the use of economy in the context of the market Hayek labels the market order a 'catallaxy' — a word derived from the Greek verb *Katallassein* which means not simply 'to exchange' but 'to admit into the community' and 'to change from enemy into friend'. To Hayek therefore, 'A catallaxy is thus the special kind of spontaneous order produced by the market through people acting within the rules of the law of property, tort and contract.'[20]

The crucial step on which catallaxy depends is the use of barter or exchange, the major condition necessary for which is laws relating to property. Once people recognise that through the process of exchange they can mutually benefit, they have no need to approve of the individual ends to which the transactions give rise. In fact in the market order there is no common purpose to which the society is oriented. This is seen as the great strength of the market order and an important condition for freedom: there is agreement on means but not ends, which makes it possible for society to reconcile the differing purposes of individuals within a catallaxy which is purely economic. 'What today connects the life of any European or American with what happens in Australia, Japan or Zaire are repercussions transmitted by the network of market relations.'[21] As a result he reaches a conclusion, which may seem astonishing, though is easily open to misinterpretation, 'The truth is that catallaxics is the science which describes the only overall order that comprehends nearly all mankind, and that the economist is therefore entitled to insist that conduciveness to that order be accepted as a standard by which all particular institutions are judged.'[22]

The simplest way to understand how catallaxy works is to imagine it to be a game. The *Oxford English Dictionary* defines a game as 'a contest played according to rules and decided by superior skill, strength or good fortune'. Viewed as a game the market has two important characteristics.

First it is a game which creates wealth through the process of production exchange and all players in the game (i.e. those supplying labour services, property and capital) are better off as a result of it. Such a positive-sum game must be contrasted with a zero-sum game in which the game to some can only be at the expense of others. The reason the market economy or catallaxy produces fresh wealth rather than simply redistributes existing wealth is critically bound up with the way in which market prices act as signals containing vital information. Current product prices convey information to producers about the likely rewards of manufacturing a particular product and current factor prices (wages, rents, interest) the likely cost of producing the product as well as the returns which labour and capital are likely to receive if they provide their services. In the market system therefore competitive prices embody information which people can use to make their decisions regarding what to produce, where to work and which skills to develop. The information embodied in such competitive prices is a measure of where resources are most needed. When individuals and corporations respond to change in prices they are simultaneously creating wealth in response to changing demands. If there is a range of technical possibilities for producing a particular commodity the function of prices is to show the least-cost solution. This enables us to say therefore that competition creates a system of prices which embodies relevant information so that the wealth created within the market order is produced at least cost. In other words, a market economy is an efficient way of producing wealth; the reason it is more efficient than a planned economy in which prices are not competitive is that prices do not convey this information. As a result planners are often in ignorance.

Second, the outcome of the game does not correspond to any ideal of distributive justice. The rules by which the game is played are known to all in advance but the result of the game is partly a matter of skill and partly of chance. If players have the freedom to act in their best interests as a response to the signals of the market place, it is simply not possible to determine the outcome of the game by reference to certain ideals of social justice. In fact any intervention with the playing of the game will distort prices, reduce the information contained in them and prevent the full adjustment which is a part and parcel of the creation of wealth in a market economy.

We are extremely indebted to Professor Hayek for his intellectual defence of the market economy: in particular for his placing it so clearly within a philosophical context which is logically consistent. All too often Milton Friedman's defence of the market economy is couched in such pragmatic terms that is obscures its true philosophical underpinnings.

Having said that, however, I have to say that from a Christian point of view the Hayekian (or Friedmanian) system is fundamentally at variance to what I conceive of as a Christian view of reality. At the most basic level there is the rejection of any purpose in the pattern of human activities, except that of the instinct for survival itself, and the acceptance of a theory of cultural evolution which explains the origin of human values. Both these propositions follow directly from an implicit agnosticism regarding the existence of God. They clash in an important way with the Christian doctrine of creation which provides both a purpose to human activity and a cultural mandate defining the terms of man's trusteeship in this world. For the Christian the source of human values is *neither* the result of genetics *nor* the product of human reason *nor* even as Hayek would have it a process of cultural selection by which certain rules of conduct become accepted and others rejected, but the revelation by God through his Word in history.

The adoption of the evolutionary point of view leads to two very important conclusions. First it guarantees a kind of harmony in the market economy. In *The Wealth of Nations,* Adam Smith showed how even though each individual pursued his own self-interest, nevertheless through the invisible hand he was led 'to promote an end which was no part in his intentions'.[23] In the same way Bernard Mandeville subtitled *The Fable of the Bees* 'Private Vices, Public Benefits' and showed how in the economy of the hive social harmony could result from each individual pursuing his own self-interest. The moral of this fable is:

> Thus every part was full of vice
> And yet the whole a Paradise
> the worse of all the multitude
> Did something for the common good.[24]

In the Hayekian view of the market economy a similar result emerges. If individuals are allowed to pursue their self-interest, if prices are allowed to respond to changes in information and if players in the game have the assurance that there exists a rule of law which guarantees their contracts, the market economy left to itself will secure the best outcome for society as a whole. The reason as we have seen is that it succeeds in employing more information than any alternative system. Intervention in the market economy can only lead to harmful results, therefore, because it will disrupt the workings of the overall economic order. However, the guaranteed harmony of economic activity resulting either from a mechanistic or biological analogy fits in awkwardly with a Christian view of man and work.

Were the Factory Acts of the early nineteenth century a disruption of the economic order?

Is anti-monopoly legislation of no value because monopolies find it difficult to survive in the long run?

Is town planning an interference with the natural growth of cities?

I find it difficult to believe that intervention is of necessity harmful. What, however, a large number of studies of the effects of regulation do show is that there are frequently unintended consequences of regulation which impose a cost on society that must be weighed against the expected benefits of the regulation.

The second conclusion which follows from this evolutionary view has to do with the concept of justice. In the Hayekian view justice is solely to do with the rules of the game. Justice is concerned with the protection of private property and the enforcement of contracts because these are essential equipment for playing the game. But a Christian view of justice is more than this. No one can read the Pentateuch and conclude that justice is just concerned with private property and the rule of law. It also relates to much wider issues such as the abuse of monopoly power, exploitation and poverty.

Consider two practical areas in which Hayek's philosophy of the market order leads him into what I consider real problems:

Pollution

Within his framework, pollution, which might be considered a cost imposed on society but not paid for by the company creating the pollution, results from a deficient system of property rights. If the ownership of rivers and lakes were as well defined as houses and factories, then the law of tort and contract would ensure that their owners were in a position to take legal action against any company which pumped effluent into them. But what would happen if the companies concerned bought up the rivers and lakes? Assume for example that Ford and General Motors between them are in a position to buy up the Great Lakes and pollute them as much as they desire in order to reduce the costs against such an action. A libertarian would have no objection to such a course of action. But a Christian certainly would because he starts from a different basis. If we assume that we are not the proprietors but the trustees of this world and that we have a deed of covenant to honour, this at once introduces certain absolutes into economic life and certain limits on the exercise of freedom. As trustees we have a responsibility to respect the natural world, which acts as a constraint on even our need to pollute it to keep costs down.

The poor

While I fully accept that the poor have become a cause by which many politicians and intellectuals can further their personal ambitions, I do nevertheless find that the Hayekian case is deficient. In a libertarian world there is no reason for the government to do anything about the poor; the matter is conveniently left to private charity. Even in Hayek's acceptance of an anti-poverty programme, the motive is purely pragmatic. It is that if governments did not do this kind of thing the probability of their interfering in the workings of the market economy would be that much greater. An anti-poverty programme therefore is an insurance premium which society has to pay to stop politicians and intellectuals from demanding greater government intervention in the workings of the market place. From a Christian point of view, however, the concern for the poor is more than just an individual matter: it is legitimately a function of government acting on behalf of society as a whole and comparable to its mandate to maintain law and order.

I believe the problem for Hayek and Friedman is even more serious than this. Professor Hayek recognises that a free-enterprise economy requires the presence of strong moral standards of a particular kind for it to work: the two crucial ones being a belief in individual responsibility and a recognition that the merit and worth of individuals do not correspond to the material rewards of the market economy. Without these he acknowledges quite candidly that the system cannot survive. He also recognises that in a free society values may develop which are alien to its very existence. In other words the modern defence of the market economy is incomplete at one point. For a market economy to work it depends on the existence of certain values. Yet we have no guarantee that a free society following a humanistic philosophy will generate the appropriate set of values to ensure this. In fact Professor Hayek is sufficiently honest to admit that the free society which we have seen grow in Europe since the Enlightenment has produced through the writings of Marx and Freud a set of values which if not renounced will destroy the civilisation itself; namely the pursuit of egalitarianism at the collective level leading to the replacement of the market economy by the planned economy and the pursuit of freedom at the personal level leading to

36

abandonment of traditional morality based on the concept of right and wrong and good and evil.

This pinpoints a fundamental weakness in the libertarian defence of a market economy. Humanism cannot necessarily generate those values which are crucial if the market economy is to survive. Since the beginnings of industrialisation these values have been provided by Christianity. A Christian view of the world emphasises those two critical moral standards which the market economy requires. In the first place it places great stress on individual responsibility. Man is created by God as a person with dignity and intrinsic worth. He is given authority over God's world. He is endowed with specific talents. The key Christian concept in all these areas is that of stewardship. We are to be responsible stewards of what God has given us. The contrast between humanist and Christian values in relation to individual responsibility struck me very forcefully recently when within the same day I happened to read *Free to Choose,* Milton and Rose Friedman's recent book in defence of economic freedoms,[25] and a sermon of John Wesley, on *'The Use of Money',* first given in London in 1748. The Friedmans' book is a polemic in favour of total economic freedom. The basis of their system is self-interest: 'Whatever it is that interests the participants, whatever they value, whatever goals they pursue.' No judgment is ever made of values or goals. Wesley's sermon provides a complete contrast. It consists of three points: gain all you can, save all you can, give all you can. In terms of individual responsibility the contrast between libertarianism and Christianity could not be greater.

In the second place, as the Christian looks at other human beings he sees them of equally infinite value and dignity because they too are made in God's image. The idea that the value and merit of individuals should be related to their income or wealth is wholly repugnant to a Christian view of the world. As a result, it is impossible to derive egalitarianism in the Marxist sense from a Biblical foundation. Equality before the law it is certainly possible to deduce: equality of opportunity it may be possible to deduce; but an egalitarianism implying equality of material reward is both logically and exegetically impossible to deduce.

The failure of humanism to generate standards conducive to the market economy can also be seen in the culture at large. Humanism has resulted in a hedonistic way of life which is turning out to be anti-intellectual and irrational — consider the works of Francis Bacon – or Sid Vicious. By contrast the market economy places emphasis on rationality, economy and optimising behaviour. Professor Daniel Bell of Harvard puts it as follows:

> The characteristic style of an industrial society is based on the principles of economics and economising: on efficiency, least cost, maximisation, optimisation, and functional rationality. Yet it is at this point that it comes into sharpest conflict with the cultural and anti-intellectual currents which are rooted in a return to instinctual modes. The one emphasises functional rationality, technocratic decision-making, and meritocratic rewards. The others, apocalyptic moods and antirational modes of behaviour. It is this disjunction which is the historic crisis of Western society. This cultural contradiction, in the long run, is the deepest challenge to the society.[26]

As we have seen, the humanist defence of the market economy is incomplete. But once we use Christian values to complete it, it renders the system logically inconsistent; because we cannot introduce Christian values on a piecemeal basis. Once we introduce Christian values at one point we are forced to introduce them at all points. Yet if we do this we undermine the whole concept of cultural evolution and the spontaneous order which underlies Hayek and Friedmans' defence of the market economy. In other words, to the extent that Christianity is seen as providing a source of values which can legitimise the market economy, those same values undermine the assumptions from which a humanistic defence of the market economy starts.

You may say at the end of all this, 'Well, where does all this leave you? Having dismissed the Hayekian argument, are you not forced into some form of socialism?' To which my answer is absolutely not — especially if you understand modern socialism too as a result of an Enlightenment view of the world.

I believe that one indisputable fact about capitalist economies is the efficiency with which markets allocate resources to create wealth. But I am also convinced that markets should not enjoy the kind of sovereign power which they are given in the Hayekian and Friedman analysis. The relevance of Christian thinking is that it puts certain limits on the market place, not on the basis that they are politically necessary to secure greater freedom in the market economy, but that they are right and desirable in themselves.

What I am arguing is that we should be trying to rescue the market economy from the libertarian philosophy with which it has become entangled and regrettably identified. The market economy has much to offer and certainly in today's world needs to be defended intellectually but only I believe if it is defended within the bounds of Christian justice.

CHAPTER 2

THE CHALLENGE OF MARXISM

Let me summarise very briefly the outline of the argument so far. We started by observing the global conflict which exists today between socialism and capitalism. We then looked at the remarkable record of capitalism in creating wealth and contrasted it with the present malaise which now seems to infect most economies of the Western world. We argued that the sickness or crisis of capitalism was not at heart a technical matter but a lack of legitimacy with respect to the system itself. We explored various explanations of the present situation — such as Schumpeter's analysis, the growth of government and the role of technology as an autonomous and primary force — and concluded that the root of the problem lay in the basic tension within humanism — the prevailing philosophy today in the Western world — namely the conflict between the desire to control and the desire to be free. This included in particular the inability of humanism as a philosophy to place adequate constraints on the exercise of freedom and also its inability to generate that set of values which is necessary if capitalism is to work. In addition, we saw that if Christianity was to be made the source of values this would create a logical inconsistency in Professor Hayek's defence of the spontaneous order.

The major conclusions are therefore that the market economy is a remarkably efficient way of creating wealth largely because it succeeds in utilising more information than alternative economic systems; that for a market economy to work, the society of which it is part needs to believe in certain kinds of values: it must lay great store by individual responsibility and also have a non-egalitarian view of what constitutes social justice; that the so called 'crisis' of capitalism results from a prevailing set of cultural values, typified by Freudianism and Marxism, which are contrary to those needed for the market economy to prosper, that humanism as a philosophy cannot guarantee to generate the appropriate values, and that Christianity can provide such values and has indeed done so during the period of industrialisation throughout much of the Western world, but in consequence the kind of market economy which is then championed is different from that currently defined by the libertarian philosophy of Professor Friedman and Professor Hayek.

The other major system of political economy prevailing in the world today is socialism. As an ideal socialism is as old as civilisation. In the tradition of Western philosophy there have always been those who longed for a society in which injustice and poverty were abolished and people able to share their material possessions. In *The Republic,* Plato outlined an ideal social system in which private property was abolished. Although great power was vested in the philosophers who were to be the rulers, their personal self-interest was not to be a source of private gain but was to be made subservient to the state. The experience of the early Christian community in Jerusalem in sharing their worldly goods is evidence for many of the material communism which is implicit in the Great Commandment 'Love your neighbour as yourself'. This view is reinforced by the writings of some of the early church fathers such as St John Chrysostom, who observed that there was no conflict over natural common property such as air, sun, water, earth, sea, light and stars or even man-made common property such as baths, cities, markets and arcades, but only over private property which created what he termed that frigid expression 'Thine and Mine'. In the medieval period numerous communal experiments were set up, a number associated with monasticism, which involved the adoption by their members of communist principles. Thomas More's vision of Utopia is that of a society in which private property would be abolished, in which the state would provide food, clothing, housing, education and medical treatment for all its members and in which the working day

41

would be only six hours in length. Godwin in his book *Political Justice* (1793), written during the time of the French Revolution, with its slogan of 'Liberty, Equality, Fraternity', argued for the abolition of private property on the ground that it retarded the moral and intellectual development of a society because of its inequality. Similarly in France in the eighteenth century writers such as Mably and Morelly, who believed passionately in the idea of equality, saw this as involving the transference of private property to the state, which could then be used to satisfy the needs of all.

Modern socialism, however, is a reaction to the Industrial Revolution which began in the second half of the eighteenth century: in particular to the advent of the machine and the factory, the rapid growth of population and urbanisation, the payment of low wages and the existence of sporadic unemployment, and to the kind of society which industrialisation created which was considered by many as inhuman, unjust and divisive. Many thinkers such as Owen, Fourier, Saint-Simon and Blanc saw the root of injustice as the competitive system of free markets, which led them to argue that the gulf between rich and poor and the exploitation of the one by the other, would not be abolished until some form of socialist state was established.

Modern socialism is dominated by Marxism. Unlike these other writers Marx analysed in detail the workings and defects of capitalism and showed a way by which the transition to a future socialist state was possible. Above everything else Marx claimed that his work had a scientific status which, as he was never tired of pointing out, was in great contrast to those whom he rather disdainfully referred to as the 'utopians'.

The success of Marxism in the modern world is quite staggering. Hardly a demonstration or revolution takes place in the world without the name of Marx being involved. Many of the basic concepts of Marxism — the class struggle, the bourgeoisie and the proletariat, the means of production, exploitation and revolution — have become part of the intellectual baggage of our age. Nearly forty per cent of people alive today live under governments which consider themselves

Marxist. Apart from the Soviet Union and its satellites in Eastern Europe (Poland, Hungary, Czechoslovakia, East Germany, Yugoslavia, Bulgaria, Rumania), Albania and China, more than twenty countries in the Third World subscribe to an official Marxist outlook (including Afghanistan, Algeria, Angola, Cambodia, Congo, Cuba, Ethiopa, Guinea-Bissau, Iraq, Laos, Libya, Mauritania, Mozambique, North Korea, Yemen, Syria, Vietman, the PLO in Palestine and SWAPO in South West Africa); and many more, although not officially Marxist, espouse various forms of socialism derivative of Marxism. In this country the influence of Marxism in the universities, trade unions and arts has reached a point where as Christians I believe we are forced to take it seriously.

There are also many Christians, especially in Latin America, and associated with international bodies such as the World Council of Churches, who are actively involved in dialogue with Marxists and who see no fundamental conflict between Christianity and Marxist. For example, Miguez Bonino who inaugurated this series of lectures, talked of his own personal discovery of 'the unsubstitutable relevance of Marxism' and went on to argue that it must be taken seriously because 'it offers a scientific, verifiable and efficacious way to articulate love historically'. And in terms of its practical record he says, 'Whatever our misgivings, it is difficult not to feel a sense of admiration and gratitude for a movement that, in less than a century, through its direct action in some areas and through indirect influence in labour movements and other social forces in others, has raised to a human condition the life of at least half of the human race.'[1]

What is Marxism?

It is important that we should be clear as to what we mean by Marxism. The task is by no means easy: not only are there the writings of Marx and Engels and then later Lenin, but also the revisionist writings of Berstein, Rosa Luxemburg and most recently the critique from within the Marxist camp from people such as Althusser and Kolakowski and other Euro-communists. Alongside theory is practice: the varying brands of Soviet communism, Stalinism, Titoism in Yugoslavia, the Dubceck experience in Czechoslovakia, not to mention the Asian communism of Mao, Vietnam and Cambodia. Despite the burgeoning of literature on this subject, I believe that we must start with the writings of Marx, Engels and Lenin, as these still remain fundamental to everything else which has followed.

If we judge the content of Marxism by the writings of Marx, Engels and Lenin it consists of three major elements: a philosophy of history, a theory of economics and a view of the state and revolution; the first derived from the work of Hegel, the second from the British classical political economy as evidenced in the writings of Ricardo, and the third from the revolutionary tradition of French socialist thinkers such as Gismondi, Proudhon, Fourrier and Saint Simon. The fact that each of these parts has such a clearly identifiable root is in no sense an attempt to belittle the originality of Marx's contribution.

Of these the most important is the philosophy of history — the attempt to explain the human predicament and place the present in the context of past and future. Marx's philosophy of history is dialectical materialism. The dialectical method of reasoning he borrowed from Engel; and we should never under-estimate its importance in being a fundamental break with the tradition of Western philosophy. The word dialectic comes from the Greek root meaning to debate or discuss. Dialectic reasoning was an attempt to arrive at truth by exploring the contradictions in an argument. Assume a particular proposition — a thesis. As the difficulties in holding to it become clear so we examine the exact opposite — its antithesis. But this also breaks down for the same reason and so we resolve the problem by taking what is valid from thesis and antithesis to form a synthesis. But the synthesis which has been established is a fresh thesis and so the whole process starts again. For example, in Marx feudalism gives rise to capitalism because of the conflict between serf and landlord. But capitalism in turn gives way to socialism because of the conflict between owner and worker. As a synthesis of feudalism and capitalism, socialism is able to take what is best from both systems and discard those institutions which are the basis of conflict. Such Hegelian logic put a new interpretation to history. History was no longer a sequence of events but a drama in which scene followed scene and act followed act, the whole process being rational, but understood only to the extent that the particular was related to the whole.

Marx's philosophy of history, however, is materialistic as well as dialectic. For Marx the material world is the ultimate reality. Human institutions and ideas are a superstructure built on economic reality. The initial and critical assumption is that because people need to work in order to live, the economic basis of a society governs all human relationships and culture. We can think of it in terms of three levels. First there are the 'productive forces' of an economy — its natural resources, technology and skills which determine the relationship between people and things. Next are the 'productive relations' of an economy — its natural resources, technology and skills which determine the relationship between people and things. Next are the 'productive relations' of an economy, namely the relationship between people as evidenced in the institution of property and the relationships of class which depend on the productive forces. The productive relations in turn given rise to the super-structure of the society, the third tier, which include its laws, religion, culture and politics, all of which in a Marxian analysis are devised to keep the dominant class in power.

In the introduction to his *Contribution to the Critique of Political Economy* Marx brings together the materialistic and the dialectic view of history. He analyses all known history in terms of five modes of production subsequent to a primitive stage of cooperation: slavery, serfdom, wage labour, an Asiatic mode and finally, socialism. After the initial primitive stage certain members of society gain control over the forces of production so permitting a minority to exploit the majority: under slavery the slave-owner exploits the slaves; under feudalism the landlords exploits the serfs; and under capitalism the bourgeoisie exploits the proletariat. But exploitation produces conflict and it is because of the conflict inherent in each stage of development that history is the unfolding of a drama in which we move from one kind of society to another and which ultimately leads to socialism. Because change occurs as a result of the social conflict resulting from the exploitation of the majority by the minority, Marx and Engels can confidently assert in the Communist Manifesto that 'the history of all hitherto existing society is the history of class struggles'. As a result history is driven not by ideas and religion but by the economic basis of our culture. The materialistic interpretation of history therefore is a dialectical method linked to a materialistic world-view and applied to human history. Marx's particular claim was that the macro-historical laws which he had discovered were not just speculative but had a scientific status. As Engels put it, 'Just as Darwin discovered the law of evolution in organic nature, so Marx discovered the law of evolution in human history'.[2]

The main purpose of Marx's economic theory is to explain the phenomenon of surplus value in the capitalism system and the reason why capitalism as an economic system cannot survive but must give way to socialism. These can be expressed in varying degrees of complexity but I shall try to keep it as simple as possible. First, let us look at surplus labour. Marx makes three key assumptions in developing the concept of surplus labour. To start with there is the distinction between exchange value and use value. Exchange value is the price of some commodity quoted in the market place. Use value is the real satisfaction yielded by the commodity. For example, if a pound of coffee sells for £3 this is its exchange value. But its use value is its power to satisfy consumer demand for some stimulant. Exchange values are dependent on the market whereas use values are not. Next is the assumption that labour alone creates value, so that the exchange value of a commodity depends on the amount of labour it takes to produce it. Finally, there is the assumption that because labour is exchanged in a market like any other commodity wages, which are the exchange value of labour, will settle at a subsistence level. The exchange value of labour is the amount needed to produce it; in other words the amount needed to keep workers alive, but only just.

From these assumptions we can readily understand surplus value. Capitalism is a system in which the means of production, plant, machinery, land, is owned by the capitalist. He is able to use capital productively because he can buy the workers' labour power and the price he pays is the subsistence wage. But if he can use labour to produce commodities greater in value than he pays the workers then he can make a profit — and it is this Marx refers to as surplus value.

Assume that the daily wage is £10 for eight hours worked, and this just equals the subsistence level. If wages were less workers would die of starvation. The exchange value of eight hours of labour will therefore be £10 and this will equal the value added by the worker to raw materials. Further, assume that due to technological improvement workers can now produce twice as much. The price the capitalism pays for labour is still only £10 per day but the value of commodities produced by labour is now £20 per day. The difference between the two is the surplus value which the capitalist can extract from the workers. As the surplus value or, as we should refer to it today, profit is reaped by the capitalist the system is unjust in that it enables the owners to exploit the workers. The very heart of Marx's analysis of capitalism therefore rests on the simple but powerful concept that profit is robbery. But capitalism is not only unjust it is inhuman: it enables the owners of capital to treat labour and human work as a commodity, which produces 'alienation'.

The existence of surplus labour is not confined to capitalism. Under slavery, the slave-owner can extort the surplus by buying the source of labour itself; and under feudalism, the landlord can use force to make the serf submit. What is unique about capitalism is that exploitation and surplus labour can exist even within a system of free labour markets, so creating the illusion that the worker is also free; but as Marx points out this is not the case.

Because of the capitalist's desire for profit and wealth Marx develops a number of arguments to show that the system cannot survive. Competition forces the owners to replace men by machines. Unemployment rises and so increases the army of industrial reserves: as a result wages are driven down even further. But as the number of machines in an economy is increased, so the long-term rate of profit is reduced. The result is a growing contradiction between the wealth of the capitalists and the poverty, oppression and misery of the masses. At last nothing can hold back the revolution — the result in his famous phrase is that 'the expropriators are expropriated'.

The third element of the Marxist approach is a view of the state and revolution. One thing about which Marx and Engels are quite adamant is the nature of the state. Whereas most theories of the state view it as providing certain services which promote the welfare of the society, they see it as an instrument of repression which is used by the ruling class to maintain the status quo. 'The state is nothing more than a machine for the oppression of one class by another.' (Marx: *Civil War in France).* [3] Because it is the product of the class struggle, it will disappear or as Engels puts it 'wither away' with the advent of socialism. Precisely what this means is not clear because presumably even in a socialist state it would have a necessary function in maintaining law and order. While Engels attempts to meet this point by stating that 'the government of persons is replaced by the administration of things' the meaning still remains unclear. [4]

One important implication of this view of the state is that injustice cannot be removed by reform, only by a revolution, and one which involves a radical change in the system, property rights, the content of education, the family, the fiscal system and so on. In the Communist Manifesto published in 1849 the major changes to be brought about by revolution were the abolition of private property in land; a heavy progressive income tax; the abolition of the right of inheritance; nationalisation of banking, transport and the media; and free education for all children in public schools. And with this went the abolition of religion itself – something which was perfectly natural in view of the changed productive relationships in society.

Three Questions of Marxism

Such then is the standard outline of Marxism. In view of the attempt by euro-communists and Latin American 'Christian Marxists' to develop a non-dogmatic form of Marxism I believe we need to ask some basic questions about what Marxism really is. I should like to consider three in particular:

(a) *Is Marxism Scientific?*

In the preface to *Capital,* Marx said, 'It is the ultimate aim of this work to lay bare the . . . law of motion of modern society.'[5] Marx's major claim for his own work was that he had discovered certain inexorable laws which operated in history and which were comparable in their workings to laws operating in the physical universe such as the law of gravity. His method was empirical: 'My results have been obtained through a completely empirical analysis founded on a conscientious and critical study of political economy.' There can be no doubt that this claim has impressed many as an important reason why his views should not only be taken seriously but accepted as true.

In my opinion the claim of scientific status for the Marxist method is misplaced. To start with, Marx was not interested in scientific prediction in the way that physics, astronomy or modern economics are concerned with prediction, but with what Professor Sir Karl Popper so aptly terms 'large scale historical prophecy'. Modern science is concerned with observation, the development of theory, the construction of hypotheses, and the testing of these hypotheses against the facts. By its very nature it is hesitant, tentative and agnostic. Predictability and falsifiability are an important part of the scientific method. If a hypothesis is falsified by the empirical evidence then it has to be changed to explain that evidence. This is hardly a description, however, of the Marxist method.

Consider the labour theory of value. It is not too strong to say that it is impossible to test Marx's thesis regarding the labour theory of value at a micro-economic level because Marx and Marxists have totally disregarded any element of profit which may result from risk-taking. In Marx, profit is the consequence of exploitation, not a return to entrepreneurial risk-taking activity. So the Marxist contention that capitalism is exploitation is not the result of carefully considered empirical evidence but of the Marxist definition of value. This is in sharp contrast to the approach of traditional neo-classical economics. Within the neo-classical framework profit is essentially a return to capital investment as a reward for the risk borne by its owners. This does not mean that exploitation cannot or does not exist. In a situation of monopoly power, the profits which a company makes will contain an element which can only be ascribed to the use of monopoly power by that company. By examining the relationship between the rate of return on capital invested in various industries and barriers to entry and exit from such industries, it is possible to test the hypothesis that monopoly power results in excessive profits. In other words, within a non-Marxist framework the ability of a company which possesses a monopoly to exploit its monopoly is something which is determined by the evidence and not as in Marxism by the way in which value is defined.

Then there are a number of predictions made in Marxist literature, such as the transition from socialism to communism, which it is impossible to subject to any meaningful test, and which are not even developed analytically. In view of these observations it is also interesting to note that there seem to be very few social scientists within communist countries who are involved in developing and testing Marxist–Leninist theory. They may be involved in planning, organising foreign trade, predicting the money needed by their economies, but few are involved in developing Marxist–Leninist theory itself.

Not only is the method not scientific but, to the extent that Marx did make certain historical prophecies which can be related to empirical evidence over long periods of time, these can

50

be examined and by and large they have not proved to be valid.

Consider the following predictions. That working-class wages would remain at subsistence level — *the fact* is that the real wage of the average worker has increased by a factor of over ten between 1900-70 in the UK and by a factor of fourteen in the US over the same period; that collective ownership of the means of production would result in an increase of wealth for the workers and so improve their lot — *the fact* is that in both Russia and Cuba it has been necessary to restore discipline in factories by introducing a military routine with the surplus value being siphoned off by the state; that communist revolutions would start in such advanced industrial countries such as Britain, France, America and Germany — *the fact* is that a socialist revolution has taken place in none of these countries; that conflicts between states are the results of capitalism and will cease under communism — *the fact* is that in the streets of Budapest and Prague, in Afghanistan and on the Soviet-Chinese border we have seen the power of the Red Army being used against fellow communists; that the income difference between capitalists and workers will rise — *the fact* is that in all industrial countries the effective after-tax, after-benefits real income gap between rich and poor has diminished; that capitalism will collapse because of its internal contradictions — *the fact* is that capitalism has not collapsed in any Western country, yet. The only prediction which it could be claimed has been validated is that the rate of profit would fall. This has happened in a number of developed countries — though not for the reasons given by Marx but primarily because of the growth of government and restrictive practices in labour markets.

(b) *Is Marxism Humanistic?*

Humanitarianism has always been one of the major motivations making for socialism. And it is certainly impossible to read Marx without acknowledging in his writings a strong humanitarian inspiration. In his early works he was very concerned with the problem of 'alienation' and the 'essence of man' and even in

Capital it is impossible not to be moved in reading his account of conditions in England during the first half of the nineteenth century. For example, he quotes a report to the Children's Employment Commissioners regarding the potteries of Staffordshire:

> William Wood, 9 years old, 'was 7 years 10 months old when he began to work'. He 'ran moulds' (carried ready-moulded articles into the drying-room, afterwards bringing back the empty mould) from the very beginning. He came to work every day in the week at 6 a.m. and left off at about 9 p.m. 'I work till 9 o'clock at night six days in the week. I have done so for the last seven or eight weeks.' Fifteen hours of labour for a child of 7![6]

Again from the report of the Commissioners in 1863, the following extract is taken from the evidence of Dr J.T. Arledge, senior physician of the North Staffordshire Infirmary:

> The potters as a class, both men and women, represent a degenerated population, both physically and morally. They are, as a rule, stunted in growth, ill-shaped, and frequently ill-formed in the chest; they become prematurely old, and are certainly short-lived; they are phlegmatic and bloodless and exhibit their debility of constitution by obstinate attacks of dyspepsia, and disorders of the liver and kidneys, and by rheumatism. But of all diseases they are especially prone to chest-disease, to pneumonia, phthisis, bronchitis, and asthma. One form would appear peculiar to them, and is known as potter's asthma, or potter's consumption. Scrofula attacking the glands, or bones, or other parts of the body, is a disease of two-thirds or more of the potters . . . That the 'degenerescence' of the population of this district is not even greater than it is, is due to the constant recruiting from the adjacent country, and intermarriages with more healthy races.[7]

As one read passages such as these one must acknowledge the

force of Merleau–Ponty's statement that 'one does not become revolutionary through science but through indignation'.

However, when this is accepted one has to say that Marx's humanitarianism is a flawed humanitarianism. For example, in correspondence Marx and Engels recognised that after power had been achieved, terror would be necessary: 'It will be necessary to repeat the year 1793. After achieving power we'll be considered monsters but we couldn't care less.'[8] In the *Communist Manifesto* the claim is made quite explicitly that the family is to be abolished, education undertaken by the state and that there is to be 'a more equitable distribution of the population over the country'.[9] It is difficult to imagine how these could ever be achieved without a flagrant disregard for basic human rights. Not only this but in the *Communist Manifesto* Marx and Engels consider the charge made against communism that there are 'eternal truths, such as Freedom, Justice, etc., that are common to all states of society. But communism abolishes eternal truths, it abolishes all religion, and all morality, instead of constituting them on a new basis: it therefore acts in contradiction to all past historical experience.'[10] They do not deny the charge, they simply assert that the social consciousness of past societies is similar because the history of all past societies is one of class antagonism. However, the communist revolution which involves the most radical change in property rights also involves 'the most radical rupture with traditional ideas'. In other words, all religion and morality are the product of the class struggle and communism does indeed *intend* to abolish eternal truths, to abolish all religion and to abolish all morality. But however can one conceive of this happening without a total disregard for humanity?

On this issue therefore, I find it curious that so many people can become excited at the humanitarianism of the young Marx while choosing at the same time to ignore the inhumanity of the more mature Marx.

If Marx's humanitarianism contains a certain ambiguity, the same cannot be said of Lenin. In his work on *The State and Revolution,* which develops an area in which Marx was somewhat vague, he displays a ruthlessness and a disregard for individual dissent which it would be difficult to match. Even after a violent revolution Lenin acknowledges:

> The proletariat needs state power, a centralised organisation of force, an organisation of violence, both to crush the resistance of the exploiters and to *lead* the enormous mass of the population — the peasants, the petty bourgeoisie and semi-proletarians — in the work of organising a socialist economy.[12]

When it comes to the organisation of industry the situation is just as terrifying.

> We the workers, shall organise large scale production on the basis of what capitalism has already created, relying on our own experience as workers, establishing strict, iron discipline backed up by the state of power of the armed workers.'[13]

I need say no more, except to underline the naivety of those who are prepared to champion the humanism of Marx in his attack on capitalism without recognising the inhumanism of Marx in proposing the socialist solution.

(c) *Is Marxism Atheistic?*

From a Christian point of view this is the most interesting question of all. The issue is to what extent Marxism is dependent on atheism. Is Marxism divisible? Can we take from Marxism certain elements without having to accept its astheistic commitment?

Although we need not spend much time on it, it is important to be clear that Marxism is atheistic. Religion was to Marx an illusion, a fantasy created by men as a result of the class struggle. In *The Holy Family,* Marx refers to socialism as the highest form of atheism: if atheism 'affirms man through the denial of God', that is, if it is the 'negative affirmation of man', then he argues that socialism is 'man's positive affirmation'.[14] As

54

BALANCE: £0.00

Total Paid: £7.00

#001   18-07-2016 4:36PM
Item(s) checked out to p11610487.

TLE: Morality and the market place
THOR: Griffiths, Brian, 1941-
RCODE: 89453101
E DATE: 08-08-16

Please keep this receipt

a result he held that 'the abolition of religion as the illusory happiness of the people is required for their real happiness'. [15] In a book published as result of the Christian–Marxist dialogue in the 1960's the Czech philosopher Vitezslaw Gardavsky, a committed Marxist, was equally clear about the matter. He put it as follows: 'Marxism is essentially atheistic, or to put it another way: it is atheism which provides the radical aspect of the Marxist philosophy of life. Without it both Marx's plan for a 'total man' and his concept of communist are equally inconceivable.' [16] That it seems to me is the heart of the matter and he has expressed it more clearly than many Christian theologians. Atheism for Marxism is not an optional extra or a mere facet but the very essence of it. It is impossible to conceive of dialectical materialism without atheism, and it is this which underlies Marxism as an ideology. It is a fundamentally atheistic ideology. At whichever point you care to touch it and examine it, the same theme emerges: God is dead, man is good, religion is illusion, reality is material, property is conflict, socialism is inevitable. In this sense I believe that Marxism is indivisible. It is impossible to select any important part of it without soon realising that its root is firmly grounded in atheism. To the extent that it is possible to separate such ideas as surplus value they seem to me totally uninteresting.

Marxism as a religious system

In view of all of this, I find myself asking what it is about the Marxist *method* which is so appealing to Latin American theologians and those Christians committed to socialism. After all, one does not have to adopt a Marxist method in order to make statements about poverty, injustice or exploitation. One can do that on the basis of Christian theology. Neither does one have to adopt such a method in order to criticise the abuse of monopoly power by governments, multi-nationals or trade unions. One can do that if one can identify excessive profits, wage levels which depend on restricting access to labour markets and gross inefficiency in the running of government enterprises.

55

Again, one does not need a Marxist framework to attack the protective tariffs and import quotas of European and North American governments. The self-interest behind such measures and the harmful effects in Third World countries are plain for all to see. Neither does one have to invoke Marxism to take history seriously and to try to understand the various forces which are at work and the way in which certain classes, institutions and pressure groups have used power to maintain inequality. When these are taken into account I have to confess that I find it difficult to understand the additional insights and explanations which the Marxist method offers.

Despite this, Marxism continues to grow as a major intellectual force in Western societies, Marxist-inspired political organisations flourish and throughout the world more and more governments fall to communism. To understand what is happening it is crucial to see Marxism not in the guise which it claims for itself — namely a scientific method — but as an ideology — a set of beliefs and ideas which help us interpret the world and provide a basis for action — which is a substitute for the religious vacuum left by the decline of Christianity in the West. Carew Hunt, who was an authority at the Foreign Office on international communism and who wrote The Theory and Practice of Communism, argues that it can only be understood in religious terms. 'For its devotees communism has the *value* of a religion, insofar as it is felt to provide a complete explanation of reality and of man as part of reality, and at the same time to give to life, as religion does, a sense of purpose.'[17] Robert C. Tucker, a Professor of Politics at Princeton, in analysing Marxian political thought expresses the view that 'from a structural viewpoint . . . Marxism invites analysis as a religious system'.[18]

Like the Christian religion, Marxism is a world-view, a *Weltanschauung;* it covers the whole of human experience and has ramifications for every area of life. It cannot be boxed into some neatly defined category as economics or sociology or politics or history. It covers all of these and more. It includes in its perspective not just economics, politics and the state, but the family, education, religion, war, women and the arts. Every conceivable phenomenon and happening can be interpreted from its perspective. In this sense it is an all-embracing world-view.

Next it is, again like Christianity, a view of history which tells the story of all known civilisations. It explains origin and destiny. It is the account of Paradise lost and Paradise regained: the primitive state with man as *homo faber* in an idyllic world; the advent of private property and the rift between oppressor and oppressed; and the final communist state in which exploitation, war and conflict will cease. It is interesting to observe, as Tucker points out, that Marx in each of his four general formulations of Marxism–in the *Paris Manuscripts of 1844,* the *German Ideology,* the *Communist Manifesto* and the preface to the *Critique of Political Ideology* — develops his exposition of doctrine as an account of the course of world history.

Implicit in this historical materialism is a view of man and an explanation of the human condition. The advent of private property is comparable to the Christian view of the Fall. There is nothing flawed about man's nature. Original sin has been replaced by original goodness, and the conflicts in human society are without exception related to the economic basis of society. Through the socialist revolution the transformation of economic life also involves the transformation of man to Kautsky's and Trotsky's 'superman', so that the Marxian revolution is comparable to the Christian view of redemption.

Lastly, it also claims 'unity of thought and practice'. It is not simply a theoretical system of thought — it is a basis for action. 'The philosophers have only interpreted the world in various ways . . . The point is to change it.' Although history is deterministic there is still the need for workers to unite and act and accept the invitation to join in the great drama of history. This is not the perspective of the dispassionate scientist or the political thinker but the missionary zeal of the revolutionary demanding participation by others.

For modern secular Western man, severed from his cultural roots by the processes of industrialisation and secularisation, Marxism makes a real appeal. It offers the qualities of religion without rejecting any of the fixed points of modernity — science, progress, agnosticism. Its vision for society is that of a reconstituted pre-industrial kind of community in which everyone knows who they are, what is expected of them and the kind of values by which they are to live. It is the utopian dream of a Christian heresy and to see it as anything less than that is to totally misunderstand it.

Marxism in Practice: The Two Triads

Fortunately our evaluation of Marxism does not have to be confined to the writings of Marx and Marxists. The Soviet Union has now been a socialist state for more than sixty years: many countries in Western Europe have been socialist for more than a quarter century; and Asia has not only the Chinese experiment in socialism but other countries in Asia, Africa and the America have experimented with socialism. It is of course an impossible task to examine the record of Marxism in such a short space as I have available. As these lectures are concerned with the role of religion I have decided to look at Marxism in terms of two triads — one of commitment and the other of outcome. Communism is committed to a large number of goals, but for our purpose three stand out: the abolition of private property, the abolition of the family and the abolition of religion. These are quite explicit in the *Communist Manifesto* as well as many other writings of many Marxist thinkers. The *Communist Manifesto* refers to 'the bourgeois clap-trap about the family and education, about the hallowed co-relation of family and child' and proudly proclaims the disappearance of the 'bourgeois family'. It is hardly surprising that such a powerful event as a revolution is necessary to uproot the social order and destroy these institutions.

As one examines the record of countries which have officially adopted the Marxist–Leninist doctrine, one tends to observe in all cases a triad of outcomes — economic inefficiency, religious persecution and political terror. The fascinating question is whether any relationship exists between the two triads. But before we look at that we must first turn to examine the record in a little more detail.

Economic Inefficiency

First, consider economic inefficiency. It would be quite wrong in thinking about the economics of socialist countries to focus exclusively on inefficiency. The Soviet Union has made great strides since the advent of socialism in 1917 and China has achieved a remarkable increase in prosperity in the years since the communists took over. Nevertheless, the collective ownership of the means of production — the nationalisation of most industries — is a central feature of communist countries. The market has been replaced by centralised planning, with the planners determining which priorities should be given to output growth in various sectors. Typically this has meant that economic policy has emphasised the primacy of industry over agriculture, investment over consumption and exports over imports. In general terms the system is bureaucratic and inflexible, with prices not conveying the kind of information which they do in a market economy and with incentives being blunted. The result tends to be low productivity, the appearance of shortages and surpluses, an exodus of skilled labour from agriculture because of its low priority and a sharp contrast between a small efficient private sector and a large inefficient public sector.

Economic inefficiency in the Soviet Union is legendary. The official state planning agency GOSPLAN sets all prices, production plans, import quotas and export targets, and allocates capital for new investment. Planning is detailed and involves the number of workers, working capital and raw materials that each firm can have. The result is surpluses and shortages and inefficiency. For example, in agriculture privately owned farm land, approximately 2–3 per cent of the Soviet Union's total farm land, produces 25 per cent of all Soviet agriculture ouptut. The USSR employs about five times as many farm workers as the US and invests about five times as much as does US farming annually, yet Soviet output is only 80 per cent that of the USA. Again like any bureaucratic system of production, risk-taking is never rewarded and hence there is no premium put on innovation. Attempts to solve this problem by economic reform run into the insuperable problem that they could only be successful if accompanied by political reforms involving denationalisation.

The situation in Poland at present is even worse. Due to the constant shortages the money economy has been transformed into a barter economy with cigarettes and alcohol being better currencies than paper money. The Finance Minister, Marian Kvzak, has warned that 'The devolution of Poland into a barter society is our greatest problem. We must stop cigarettes from becoming money and money from becoming nothing.' Empty shops and a flight from money to goods is a striking epitaph to a Marxist economy which is granted even the slightest degree of freedom.

Religious Persecution

I shall devote very little space to this subject. While persecution varies in intensity from country to country and over time within one country, I can think of no Marxist–Leninist government which has not as a matter of official policy harassed, discriminated against and persecuted religious minorities. In some cases at some times this has led to ruthless persecution with many deaths (USSR in the 1930s and China in the 1950s).

More generally it has meant that although religious freedom is formally guaranteed by the constitution, yet Bibles are unobtainable in bookshops, the printing of Bibles is forbidden, seminaries are rigidly controlled by the state, religious education in schools has been virtually eliminated, church publishing and information is under government control and Christians are discriminated against in gaining admission to colleges and in seeking professions of their choice. Well documented and detailed evidence is provided in the journal *Religion in Communist Lands*.

However, the most grotesque and bizarre feature of communism is the systematic use of political terror. Referring to the Terror under Robespierre, Marx was quite clear: 'It will be necessary to repeat the year 1793.' And the repetitions have been many. In an article in *Figaro* in 1978 Jean-Pierre Dujardin collected together the best-researched estimates of lives lost under communism: it was based on studies such as Robert Conquest's classic analysis of Stalin's purges *The Great Terror,* Professor Kuganov's seminal study of liquidations based on a detailed demographic survey of Russia's population between 1939 and 1959 and the detailed work done by Professor Richard Walker in a report commissioned by the US Senate and published in 1971. The human cost of communism is put at the staggering figure of 143 million dead. And this figure excludes the recent murder of 2½ million Cambodian citizens by Polpot. Obviously the figure is subject to a margin of error. Even if one is as generous as possible regarding the size of the error, the figure would still turn out to be several tens of millions of lost lives.

At the same time there are also the refugees who have escaped from China, East Germany, North Korea, North Vietnam and Angola. Since 1945 this figure is put at 12 million and we have recently seen dramatic examples of the same desperate remedy by the boat people of Vietnam and those escaping from Cuba.

THE HUMAN COST OF COMMUNISM[12]

1. Human cost of communism in USSR (1917–59)	66,700,000
2. Human cost of communism in USSR since 1959 (minimum estimate)	3,000,000
3. Human cost of communism in China	63,784,000
4. Massacre of Katyn	10,000
5. German civilians killed during expulsions of 1945–6	2,923,700

6. Cambodia (April 1975–April 1978)	2,500,000
7. Suppression of uprisings in E. Berlin, Prague, Budapest, Baltic states 1945–75	500,000
8. Communist aggression in Greece, Malaysia, Burma, Korea, Philippines, Vietnam, Cuba, Black Africa, Latin America	3,500,000
	142,917,700

In the light of these facts, the interesting question is whether there exists any relationship between the two triads — on the one hand the abolition of private property, religion and the family and on the other economic inefficiency, religious persecution and political terror. As a Christian my answer is a categorical yes. Communism not only declares that God is dead but savagely tears him to pieces. The *Communist Manifesto* sets out unequivocally to destroy the very institutions which God created as the basis for the social order. It should therefore come as no surprise that inefficiency, persecution, and terror are the order of the day in Marxist countries. Solzhenitsyn in his *Warning to the Western World* says, 'There is no need to think of the Gulag Archipelago as an Asiatic distortion of a noble ideal. It is an irrevocable law.' Once the state arrogates to itself the power to decide on all economic matters it is but a short step to the physical direction of labour. How else could they achieve their objectives? I would go as far as to argue that, however well-intentioned and humanitarian the people who undertake a socialist revolution, the logic of their ideology, which is of necessity reflected in the institutions which they create, makes totalitarianism inevitable.

What about Euro-Communism?

There are many committed Marxists who recognise the horror of the Soviet Union but who nevertheless feel that a Marxist state can be established without a loss of freedom.

Since the mid-seventies the expression euro-communism has

been used to describe the Communist Party of Italy, France and Spain. These parties claim that they are different from traditional Marxist–Leninist parties in three major respects: they are critical of certain aspects of the Soviet Union; they are independent of Moscow so that if they were to win an election and form a government they would not be Soviet puppets; and they claim that it is possible to implement communism and maintain traditional democratic institutions. In defence of these they point to their abandoning one of the key phrases of Soviet Marxist–Leninism, 'proletarian internationalism', which is a way of talking about Soviet domination of world communism and also of Marx's expression 'dictatorship of the proletariat' which would be contrary to the claim that communism is compatible with democracy. One of the key themes of George Marchais, the leader of the French Communist Party, is, ' "It will be different in France," people say to us, "but what you propose is quite different from what happens in socialist countries today." They are right! It will be different! We follow our own way, the way which fits in with the conditions of our time and our country.'

First, the internal organisation of euro-communist parties still remains that of democratic centralism. That is they are fundamentally undemocratic and decisions are made by the central committee of the party. *Second,* no euro-communist parties have renounced the doctrine of economic collectivisation. But as we have seen, this is at the very heart of the problem of the survival of free institutions, because if this policy is pursued it would be impossible to stop the drift to totalitarianism. *Third,* on the fundamental issues of foreign policy, although they claim independence they are forced to follow the Moscow line. Imagine a war between the West and the USSR. In such an event Radice, one of the leaders of the Italian Communist Party summed it up. 'If there is an imperialist aggression with the avowed objective of rolling back socialism, we would feel entirely absolved of any obligation of loyalty to the defensive character of NATO and take the side of the Soviet Union.' In any case it remains very doubtful, whatever the view of liberals within these parties, whether the pro-Soviet elements would allow any fundamental rejection of Soviet policy.

Experiments in Democratic Socialism: The Case of Allende's Chile

In some countries Marxists have come to power either constitutionally or through nationalist liberation movements as opposed to revolution. As a consequence, the government starts out with a legitimacy based on the will of the people. Typically, these governments talk on the one hand of establishing socialism, and on the other of wanting to work within the constraints of a democratic constitution. In September 1970, Salvador Allende's left-wing Popular Unity coalition won the presidential election in Chile and proceeded to implement a Marxist economic programme. The following year, Fidel Castro, in visiting the country, said, "Chile is like a good movie — you never want to leave.' When a movement called Christians for Socialism started in 1972, they chose to have their inaugural meeting in Santiago and received a message from the President assuring them that 'Divisions today are not on the religious level or on the level of philosophic ideas: the real division is between imperialism and dependent countries.' In September 1973, Allende was ousted in a military coup and the experiment in democratic socialism stopped. Not only is this episode interesting in itself, but it also contains important lessons which can be applied to similar attempts at implementing Marxism within a democratic framework.

President Allende took office at the end of a period of economic recession. In the previous four years GNP had grown at an average rate of about 3 per cent per annum which was lower than the preceding years and unemployment had reached a peak of 8.3 per cent in 1970. Throughout the period the balance of payments had improved noticeably, the government's deficit had been reduced by 1970 to only 15 per cent of current government revenue, investment in real terms

64

was rising and the rate of inflation averaged between 25–30 per cent per annum. By the time, however, that President Allende was ousted in September 1973, the situation had been dramatically reversed. Even though the prices of many of the goods which were used in constructing the retail price index were subject to government control, the official consumer price index increased between January 1970 and September 1973 by 119 per cent and, using this same index, the official rate of inflation in the fourth quarter of 1973 was over 500 per cent. In the month of October alone, prices rose by 87 per cent. Attempts to estimate the 'true' price rise over the same period suggest an increase in the price level of 2,531 per cent, which accords with an estimate of the economic department of the University of Chile of a rise in the black market price of the dollar of 3,600 per cent! Over the same period, real wages fell by 18.5 per cent (in 1970 it was estimated by DEPLAN, the government planning agency, that there was 25 per cent excess capacity in the economy), the government deficit increased rapidly until in 1973 it was greater than the revenue of the government, the rate of growth of fixed investment fell dramatically and the balance of payments was in deficit, on both current and capital account, throughout the whole period. The inflation was a monetary phenomenon. In 1971 money growth rose to 113 per cent; in 1972 to 152 per cent, and the estimated figure for 1973, before the collapse of the government, was between 450 and 500 per cent. Corresponding to the dramatic acceleration in the stock of money was an equally dramatic acceleration in the rate of inflation. Over 1971 the rate of inflation was only 22 per cent, over 1972 it was 163 per cent and throughout 1973, 508 per cent.

The major factor making for such an enormous increase in the money supply was the equally dramatic rise in government expediture and the inability of the government to raise tax revenue by a corresponding amount. In 1970 the actual deficit measured in terms of millions of 1969 escudos was 2,317, in 1971 it was 8,390, in 1972 it was 10,010 and in 1973, 12,348. What is interesting is that the actual deficits of 1971 and 1972 turned out to be over twice the planned deficits for those years and the actual deficit of 1975 three times the projected deficit for that year. The major stimulus to increased government spending was the financing of the Area of Social Ownership, the publicly owned part of the economy, which grew rapidly during the tenure of the government, as large areas of industry and agriculture were nationalised. The reason for the deficit was the enormous increase in government expediture and the inability of the government either to increase the rates of existing taxes or raise new taxes. This was because these changes required the approval of Congress, which was not granted because it was controlled by opposition parties. In the 1970 election, Allende won 36 per cent of the poll. Second was the conservative candidate of the Nationalist Party with 34 per cent and third a radical reformer from the Christian Democrat Party with 28 per cent of the poll. Even after the mid-1973 elections when the Popular Unity Coalition increased their share of the vote to 44 per cent, at no time did Allende have an overall Congressional majority.

The economic and political consequences of the Chilean inflation were made worse as a result of the widespread use of controls. One sector in which effects of controls were evident was agriculture. Because of controls over food prices, an enormous food shortage was created, which was then partly alleviated by substantial increases in food imports — in 1972 food imports rose by 44 per cent. Another consequence of the artificially stimulated excess demand for food was the creation of black markets. In order to ensure the supply of food to these markets the government established buying agencies at a national level and prohibited the transport of agricultural products between different provinces without official authorisation. The uncertainty which the food shortage created also led to the hoarding of food by those fortunate enough to be able to purchase it. As a result of controls and the land reforms which the government carried out, agricultural output slumped. Cultivated land decreased during 1972-3 by 22.4 per cent — the lowest level for forty years.

Another area in which the government introduced controls was over foreign payments. Severe import controls were introduced and were one of the factors explaining the slump in industrial production in 1973. As a result of the controls it was impossible for certain firms to obtain raw materials and replacements, for which no domestic substitutes were available. This generated bottlenecks which in turn led to a fall in industrial production. The truckers' strike during July and August 1973 was also largely motivated by controls — the shortages of spare parts for their trucks, official discrimination against them in favour of state-run firms, and the fact that the charges which they could make were fixed by the government but not adjusted to take into account the rapid rate of inflation. Support was evident from small business people whose firms were bankrupt, housewives who found themselves queuing for the basic necessities and civil servants and skilled workers whose salaries had fallen in real terms as a result of the inflation.

By the time Allende was ousted in September 1973 therefore, the economy was in a state of chaos. The government's finances and the creation of money were out of control. Inflation was raging, shortages and queues were everywhere. Output was falling, strikes were growing and the only response of the government was to impose more and more controls at home and blame foreign capital and the US in particular for the mess which it had itself created.

It is as well to be clear about two charges made by the Left to explain Allende's downfall. One puts it down to American intervention: in particular the role of ITT, the supplying of arms to the Chilean armed forces and the cutting-off of economic aid to Chile. Two facts about ITT are not open to question; that the company considered ways of preventing Allende assuming power and that they lobbied Washington to get rid of him when he became President. So far, there is no evidence whatever that the ITT proposals were adopted by the CIA, the Pentagon or any other body in the US. On the second point, the US military continued to maintain contact with their Chilean opposite numbers and to continue supplying arms (imagine the outcry if they had stopped) but again there is no evidence whatever of any US military involvement in the 1973 coup. The US did cut off aid to Chile after the Chilean government had nationalised the copper mines with token compensation, but was not able to prevent other Western governments from continuing to extend aid. It would be difficult to argue that this had a major effect on the Chilean economy. I feel sure that there were many in Washington who were dismayed when Allende was first elected and delighted when he was removed, but to suggest that his downfall was the result of a US conspiracy is just fanciful.

The other explanation put forward for Allende's defeat was the role of the 'privileged', the 'bosses' and the ruling elite — the transport workers' strikes which inflicted serious damage on the economy and are referred to as the 'bosses' strikes'.

As the inflation worsened and as numerous small private entrepreneurs found themselves discriminated against by government controls, they went on strike. The reasons for the lorry drivers' strike have already been given. It was joined by small shopkeepers, doctors, dentists, lawyers, and airline pilots not from some conspiracy but because of the damaging re-distributive effects of inflation which all were experiencing. The most serious of all strikes — in the copper mines — came from blue-collar workers. To try to devise some hidden hand at work here when there is a perfectly good explanation is to ignore the appalling mismanagement of the Chilean economy which was taking place.

What conclusions can be drawn from this experiment in democratic socialism? First, that any attempt to implement a Marxist economic programme even on a relatively modest scale in a country which still has a large degree of freedom is doomed to catastrophe. To implement wholesale public ownership, public spending must rise sharply. If taxes rise simultaneously there is the prospect of a major disincentive effect on output or of growth in the black economy. If the government sells bonds to pay for its spending, interest rates rise and the private sector is squeezed. If the central bank is forced to print money then inflation begins to take off and the economy languishes. At the same time the private sector and foreign capital lose confidence in the ability of the government to manage its affairs and so people prefer not to invest but take funds out of the country. Import controls only make the situation worse and help create a siege economy situation. Second, the political response to a rapid deterioration in the economy implies a greater probability of a coup d'état or a battening down of the hatches by the government. If democratic elections still exist, the chances are that the government will be voted out of office. In this respect an important lesson from Allende's experiment is that the decision to abolish private property inevitably results in the erosion of economic and political freedom also.

Conclusions

To conclude on such a vast subject as this is not easy but I would like to make the following points. First, the concern of socialists with justice is a rebuke to many of us in the West who tend to be far too complacent in accepting the status quo and much which is unjust which goes with it. Second, Marxism is a challenge to the liberal view of economics. It forces us to see man in total and forces us to recognise the limitations of a positivist view of the social sciences. Third and more important, the most outstanding fact about Marxism in the modern world is its almost total failure in economic and political terms. Wherever it has been tried it has manifestly failed either to produce prosperity or to protect human rights. In the last chapter we saw that the crisis of capitalism resulted from the crisis of humanism — the inability to resolve the basic tension between freedom and control. Capitalism suffers because of inadequate limits on the exercise of freedom. But Marxism too has its roots in humanism. It makes freedom subservient to control; and as a result, communism in practice suffers from an inability to put adequate constraints on the urge to control. At a time when there is such disaffection from socialism among many thinking people it is ironic to see the Christian churches attempting to accommodate themselves to what is at heart a devilish religion and ideology. On this the last word must be Solzhenitzyn's: 'There are many who are aware that communism is an evil and menace to the world, but who have nevertheless failed to grasp its implacable nature . . . Two mistakes are especially common. One is the failure to understand the radical hostility of communism to mankind as a whole — the failure to realise that communism is irredeemable, that there exist no "better" variants of communism: that it is incapable of growing "kinder", that it cannot survive as an ideology without using terror and that consequently to co-exist with communism on the same planet is impossible. Either it will spread, cancer-like, to destroy mankind, or else mankind will have to rid itself of communism.'[13]

CHAPTER 3

IS CHRISTIANITY RELEVANT?

At the beginning of this book we observed the global conflict which exists today between socialism and capitalism. We looked at the remarkable record of capitalism in creating wealth and contrasted it with the present malaise which now seems to infect most economies of the Western world. We argued that the sickness or crisis of capitalism was not at heart a technical matter, but a lack of legitimacy with respect to the system itself. We explored various explanations of the present situation — such as Schumpeter's analysis, the growth of government and the role of technology as an autonomous and primary force — and concluded that the root of the problem lay in a basic tension within humanism (the prevailing philosophy today in the Western world) namely between the desire to control and the desire to be free. This resulted in the inability of humanism as a philosophy to place adequate constraints on the exercise of freedom and also its inability to generate that set of values which is necessary if capitalism is to work. As a result we argued that the so called 'crisis' of capitalism results from a prevailing set of cultural values, which are alien to those required if the market economy is to survive, typified by a counter-culture which eschews the traditional distinction between good and evil and right and wrong, and which is committed to establishing an egalitarian economic system.

Next we considered the major alternative form of economic system, namely a socialism based on Marxism. We argued that Marxism could be broken up into three elements: a philosophy of history, a theory of economics and a view of the state and revolution. We then considered its claim to be scientific, humanistic and atheistic; concluding that it was more accurate to describe it as an ideology than a science, that its humanitarianism was very real yet flawed, and that its atheism was fundamental to an understanding of the ideology. We noted that in practice there was a connection between two triads — the Marxist commitment to abolish the family, private property and religion and the seeming inevitability of economic inefficiency, religious persecution and political terror. Because Marxism like humanism is also the product of an Enlightenment view of the world, the practical problems of both capitalism and communism are seen to have a common origin — namely the inability of humanism as a philosophy to resolve the basic tension between freedom and control. Capitalism suffers from inflation, instability, pollution and injustice because of inadequate limits on the exercise of freedom. Communism suffers from the direction of capital and labour and state control of the family, religion, education and the arts, because of inadequate limits on the urge to dominate.

In other words the root of the problems with both systems is a religious one. It is the irreconcilable contradiction inevitable in humanism because of its false assumptions in constructing a world-view. The tragedy, however, is that neither system recognises the true cause of its problem. From a Christian point of view therefore the root cause of the crisis of capitalism is not bigger government *or* more complex technology *or* even defects in the system of property rights, but certain false values on which it is based. Similarly Marxism is wrong in seeing the problems of modernity as exclusively the result of the capitalist system and attempting to account for the behaviour of a Stalin or a Khruschev, or a Mao Tse-tung or a Hoxha in terms of the cult of personality while at the same time ignoring the lack of moral constraints on the exercise of power in modern Marxist states.

Accepting, therefore, that the inadequacies of both capitalism and Marxism are inextricably connected with religion, has Christianity anything to offer? Is Christianity relevant to matters of political economy. Does it have anything to say about economic values and institutions? Can it point us as a nation in certain directions? Can it help Third World countries as they are forced to choose between capitalism and Marxism both of which seem to have unattractive features? If I did not believe that the answer to these questions was in each case a resounding yes I would have found it very difficult to give these lectures. I believe that the Christian faith provides us with a unique perspective on matters of political economy which is not confined to issues of personal honesty and motivation, but which is also related to the basic institutions and goals of our societies.

Common Approaches to Economics and Christianity

Before, however, I examine in more detail my own personal views on this subject I would like to set them against the background of alternative approaches.

The first assertion I would like to discuss is that the connection between the Christian faith and economic matters is indirect. It is an approach which is developed at some length by Professor Ronald H. Preston. 'We cannot move directly to particular fixed ethical conclusions from either the Bible or Natural Law.'[1] Although the traditional approach is precisely this, Professor Preston argues that it is no longer adequate because of the effects of secularisation on Western society. Traditional teaching is relative rather than fixed because of our greater understanding of the limits imposed by culture. The decline of religion and the growth of the scientific world-view have meant that 'Both the natural sciences and the social sciences have succeeded in gaining a proper autonomy from ecclesiastical control.'[2] Nevertheless anyone who wishes to say something in this area must draw on the results of research undertaken by the social sciences and so must accept their autonomy. Using this approach he attacks in particular those theologians earlier in the century who criticised capitalism and who equated the Kingdom of God with socialism.

While I think he is right to criticise those who propounded a social gospel earlier in the century he does so for the wrong

73

reason. The theology of the social gospel was inadequate because of its neglect of the importance of personal salvation and its neglect of the importance of sin in considering the structures of society. It should not however be criticised because of its attempt to relate the gospel as directly as possible to the world in which we live. The problem with Professor Preston's method is his assumption that the social sciences have a legitimate independence from Christian theology. To the extent that the Church no longer dominates Western thought this is of course correct. But because modern social science is itself the result of an Enlightenment view of the world I believe that the task of the Christian is to question the validity of such autonomy. As Christians we must not be intimidated by secularisation: if we are, we have nothing distinctive to say. In fact if we took this argument to its logical conclusion we would of course be forced to reject Christianity itself, which in its fundamentals is a pre-modern view of the world. The wide acceptance of secularisation is not a strong enough reason for us to cease applying Biblical social teaching as directly as possible to the world in which we live. To the extent that Professor Preston is warning us of the dangers of oversimplification and bad hermeneutics then we do well to listen to him.

A second approach is to argue that the Christian faith is something intensely personal, concerned with individual spirituality and not something which has a social dimension concerned with the affairs of this world. Based on the idea that the service of God is incompatible with the service of Mammon and that true spirituality involves the renunciation of the material world, this view produces a dualism in which one set of principles applies at the level of personal relationships and an altogether different set to the affairs of the world. Taken to an extreme view it results in monasticism and the creation of Christian communes. I believe it to be a defective understanding of the Christian doctrine of creation and also as we shall see later, of the social dimension of the gospel.

A third approach which grows out of the Latin American situation is the 'Theology of Liberation'. The twin starting points for this view are the widespread injustice and oppression which exist today in Latin America and which are then analysed sociologically with a Marxist framework, together with the fact that in the Incarnation God has declared his intention to liberate all people from every kind of slavery and injustice. The perspective of liberation theology is historical. History is the process by which the liberation which Christ proclaimed will be made effective for the whole world. Because therefore God is working within the sphere of history, great emphasis is made of the 'primacy of action'. For example, *Gutierrez* can say that:

> To work, to transform this world, is to become a man and to build the human community; it is also to save. Likewise, to struggle against misery and exploitation and to build a just society is already to be part of the saving action, which is moving towards its complete fulfillment. All this means that building the temporal city is not simply a stage of 'humanisation' or 'pre-evangelisation' as was held up until a few years ago. Rather it is to become part of a saving process which embraces the whole of man and all human history. Any theological reflection on human work and social praxis ought to be rooted in this fundamental affirmation.[3]

I find two critical problems with this approach; its epistemology and its soteriology. By emphasising the 'primacy of action' what these theologians are really saying is that we do not know — indeed we cannot obtain knowledge except through praxis. The only valid starting point is the situation. This is precisely the method of the Marxist. Miguez Bonino sums up their views on this point as follows:

> They are saying in fact that there is no truth outside or beyond the concrete historical events in which men are involved as agents [and] there is therefore no knowledge except in action itself, in the process of transforming the world through participating in history.[4]

I believe that this view is explicitly a rejection of the importance of the Biblical revelation.

Next there is these theologians' view of salvation. Salvation is viewed purely in termporal terms. It is synonymous with the quest for justice. As the quote from Gutierrez shows, the struggle to build a just society is itself part of the process of salvation. Another Latin American writer, José P. Miranda, goes even further and argues that God 'is knowable exclusively in the cry of the poor and the weak who seek justice'. This is a far cry from our Lord's proclamation of the good news in which salvation is primarily spiritual and moral, not political and social, and in which the act of deliverance *itself* is wholly related to the reform of social and political institutions even though it should have an implication in that area.

The Bible and the Elements of a Biblical Input

It is against this background therefore that I would like to state what I see as the relevance of Christianity to political economy. In so doing I lay great emphasis on the Biblical text because I consider the Scriptures to be our ultimate authority in matters of doctrine and life. This is in no sense an attempt to deny the importance of church tradition or the use of human reason. But when there is a conflict between the Bible and either tradition or the assumption of theology I believe we should assert the supremacy of the written Word if for no other reason than that our Lord adopted precisely this approach with respect of the Old Testament. He regarded the Old Testament text as an accurate historical record, as authoritative in matters of doctrine and ethics, and as inspired of God. In the matter of relating Christianity to economics this is a vitally important assumption because we face great cultural and intellectual pressure as Christians to adopt a form of dualism in which we substitute Smith or Marx or Friedman or Hayek for the divine revelation as the ultimate authority in this area of life. To the extent that we do this I believe we are guilty of a modern form of syncretism which is of necessity unsatisfactory.

For many of those who do take the text seriously however, Christian teaching on the subject of wealth is summed up *either* by one of the easily remembered phrases from the Gospels such as 'Sell all that you have and distribute to the poor, and you will have treasure in heaven' (Lk 18:22) or 'You cannot serve God and Mammon' (Lk 16:13) or that 'It is easier for a camel to go through the eye of a needle than for a rich man to enter the Kingdom of God' (LK 18:25) *or* by the way in which the members of the Jerusalem Church as recorded in Acts of the Apostles shared their wealth according to the principle 'From each according to his ability, to each according to his need'.

The problem with extracting one of the sayings of Jesus or using the example of the Jerusalem Church as a model for contemporary society is that the whole of the Old Testament is neglected. Professor Gordon Dunstan is correct in arguing that 'The fundamentals of Christian social doctrine are written in the Old Testament — the Gospel had a different purpose.' It is impossible to understand the New Testament and the teachings of Jesus without understanding the Old Testament.

The Old Testament lays down the fundamentals of a Christian social ethic in three major ways. *First,* it explains the nature and purpose of creation, which has implications for our view of the physical universe, our attitude to work and the objects of economic life. *Second,* the cataclysmic effects of the Fall introduce us to the problem of scarcity and imbalance in the world as well as the impossibility of creating some economic Utopia. And *third,* the various laws which make up the Mosaic Code as part of God's covenant with the Hebrew nation, set the framework for a system of political economy. These laws are quite explicit and cover such issues as property rights, the regulation of the capital market, monopolistic price and wage setting, taxation and the redistribution of income and wealth. Although they are enunciated in the Old Testament in the context of a primitive agricultural society they nevertheless embody principles of lasting value. By contrast the New Testament is a record of the Incarnation and the establishment of the Kingdom of God, and as such is concerned primarily with the ethics of those claiming citizenship in the new Koinonia and the quality of their life there.

By using the text of Scripture I believe there are five major elements which enter into a Christian view of political economy — the understanding of Creation and Fall, the political economy of Israel, the coming of the Kingdom and the teaching of Jesus, the life of the Early Church and the eschatalogical hope.

Creation and the Fall

The starting point for any Christian view of economic life is our view of the physical world. To the Christian the natural world is not the result of some accident or chance event but of a deliberate act of creation. It is the intended consequence of a conscious act. In the words of Genesis, God said 'Let there be . . . ' and there was. In fact when God created this world he is described as working (Genesis 2:13), and frequently the world is said to be the work of his hands.

The Creator is revealed to us as a rational, moral, feeling person, capable of making choices. Although independent of his creation he is nevertheless continually involved in its maintenance. The creation therefore is not like some frictionless machine, which once set in motion carries on until stopped, but something which is dependent on the continuing work of its Creator. This is important because according to Genesis, man alone of the created world is made in the image of God. This gives man great dignity. God's image in man implies that he too is a rational, moral, feeling person capable of making choices. Not only that but part of his very raison d'être, like that of his Creator, is to work. The fourth commandment is very explicit that six days of every week are for work and one for rest. In a Christian view, therefore, work is not just necessary in order to live but the result of an irrepressible drive which is rewarding in its own right. I am never surprised when after a holiday a colleague or neighbour tells me 'I had a very nice holiday but I must say it's nice to get back to work'. The

Christian view is that work is as natural a part of our lives as food, sex, worship and leisure.

There is, however, another side to the picture which derives from the Fall. The tragedy of man is that he declares himself autonomous of God and in consequence is condemned to live East of Eden. Part of the judgment is that the whole productive process is fractured and that in particular work now assumes an element of drudgery and toil, regardless of whether that work is manual, non-manual, skilled, unskilled, managerial or professional. While it would be quite wrong to use this as a justification for the existence of certain exceptionally laborious jobs, it is also quite wrong to regard stress, tedium and alienation simply as the result of advanced technology and modern capitalism and to hope with the Marxist that by changing certain structures we can achieve some Utopia. The Fall not only affects work: it also affects our preferences, appetites and wants. It introduces, to use the Biblical expression, covetousness. In other words the Fall affects ends as well as means. It is not too strong to say that the ultimate economic problem — choice under conditions of scarcity — results from this radical rupture in the natural word and in human personality.

The context in which man is created to work is controlled by a specific mandate. The Genesis account is again very clear: 'And God blessed them, and God said unto them, Be fruitful, and multiply, and replenish the earth, and subdue it; and have dominion . . . over every living thing' (Gen. 1:28) and is repeated to Noah (after the Flood) in a virtually identical form. In Psalm 8 a similar theme emerges. After considering the mystery of creation, the Psalmist writes of man: 'Thou madest him to have domination over the works of thy hands; thou hast put all things under his feet.' These verses suggest very clearly that God created the physical world for our use and pleasure, with sufficient resources for our needs and with the specific commission to harness the resources of the natural world for our benefit. In terms of man's relationship to nature the key idea here is that of dominion. Man has dominion over the natural world. It is important to notice that he is not granted sovereignty. He cannot do just as he pleases. He has no mandate to violate and transgress the natural world. He must respect it, recognising that it is God's creation and that he exercises dominion as a trustee but does not possess exclusive proprietory rights as owner.

If we accept therefore that man is created with a desire to work, subject to a charge to control and harness the earth, it follows that the process of wealth creation is something intrinsic to a Christian view of the world. It is interesting in this respect to compare the Christian view with that of other religions. The two key features of a Christian view are that there is no essential dichotomy between the physical world and the spiritual world and that man is given authority over nature. Consider the Greek philosophers. In the Greek philosophy the physical world had the status of a deity to be feared and worshipped, which not surprisingly was a great constraint to the development of technology and the exercise of dominion over nature. More recently, in many primitive societies, where animism has been practised, it would have been considered sacrilege to bring nature under control. Even in India today, where certain animals are considered sacred and where the life of the spirit and contemplation take precedence over the development of the material world, this is an important handicap to the development of the Indian economy. It is no accident that the rise of science and technology and subsequently industrialisation and the process of wealth creation followed the acceptance of an explicitly Biblical view of the world in which manual work was not considered contemptible and in which man was delegated the task of managing the world's resources for his benefit.

The Political Economy of Israel in the Old Testament

As Christians, our approach to the Old Testament is frequently selective: we value the Ten Commandments as a basic for public morality, the psalter as a help in public worship and the record of the lives of men and women of faith as examples from which we can learn. We rarely see the Old Testament as a whole and little attention is paid to the system of political economy which is set up under divine instruction in the Pentateuch. It is important for us to consider whether it contains principles which are of value for us today.

The story of the Hebrews is of a nomadic tribal people who settled the Holy Land — a depopulated fertile agricultural area. The key to the whole of their social, economic, political and religious institutions is the concept of the covenant: an all-embracing agreement which was given by God at Mount Sinai. It was central to the practices and the institutions of the nation. Frequently we abstract from this covenant by singling out the Ten Commandments and ignoring much of the remainder of the Mosaic code. In the text of Exodus, however, it is difficult to make such a break. What follows in the rest of Exodus and the Pentateuch and indeed throughout the remainder of the Old Testament is of interest on two counts. First the system which develops on the basis of the covenant includes inter alia a complex set of property rights, income transfer mechanisms, and restrictions on the capital and labour markets, in addition to a set of values and prescriptions which prove a rigorous test of motives. Although the structure which is presented is an ideal — similar indeed to the Ten Commandments, nevertheless in the same way that the Ten Commandments are relevant to our legal system so the principles which underlie the Pentateuch are relevant to economic life — principally because they express universal truth. Second, the principles which underlie the Pentateuchal economy are found elsewhere in Scripture, thus demonstrating unity of Biblical thinking.

First let us consider the system of property rights. Property law is familial. The primary aim of land law was the preservation of families as viable economic units. God gives each family an inheritance for its economic livelihood which is inalienable. As far as possible the inheritance was to be preserved entirely. The mechanism for initially allocating the land between families involved two principles: each family received a proportion in relation to its size and the particular allocation depended on the drawing of lots. The intention therefore was to have equal per capita distribution. However all property belongs to God, 'The Land is mine and you are coming to it as strangers and pilgrims' (Gen. 25:23) and so property rights are circumscribed by legal requirements: the responsibility to leave gleanings of corn and grapes for the poor, the right of a person to eat corn and grapes when passing through a field or vineyard, the requirement that the land be fallow during the Sabbatical year.

Next, the system contained a very sophisticated method of taxation and income redistribution. We are used to measuring time in decades and centuries and millennia. However in the Pentateuch the base number is seven. Based on the seven days of creation there are seven days to a week and the Hebrew calendar is then made up of a cycle of seven years (each seventh year being the Sabbatical year) and seven cycles of seven years (with each fiftieth year being a year of Jubilee). Tithes were simply proportional taxes levied on the output of the land and herds and used to support the Levites or to be set aside for the poor — widows, orphans, etc. Each year of the cycle the first tithe was paid to the Levites (with the exception of the Sabbath) and on the third and sixth year of the cycle the second tithe was a poor tithe. The income level which one needed to qualify to receive part of this tithe is unclear and would have most likely been decided by Levitical administration based on custom. It was a simple social security system.

Redistribution was also effected in other ways. 'If your brother becomes poor, and sells part of his property, then his next of kin shall come and redeem what his brother has sold' (Lev. 25:25). Incidentally, in this context brother here does not refer exclusively to another member of the Jewish nation. The gleaning laws by which the corners of the field were to be left to the gleaners was again a straightforward income transfer. In this case the text is interesting. 'When you reap the harvest on your land, you shall not reap your field to its very border, neither shall you gather the gleanings after your harvest. And you shall not strip your vineyard bare, neither shall you gather the fallen grapes of your vineyard; you shall leave them for the poor and for the sojourner: I am the Lord your God' (Lev. 19:9).

'When you reap your harvest in your field, and have forgotten a sheaf in the field, you shall not go back to get it; it shall be for the sojourner, the fatherless and the widow; that the Lord your God may bless you in all the work of your hands. When you beat your olive trees, you shall not go over the boughs again; it shall be for the sojourner, the fatherless and the widow. When you gather the grapes of your vineyard, you shall not glean it afterward; it shall be for the sojourner, the fatherless, and the widow' (Deut. 24:19-21).

In addition to the tithing system and the gleaning laws, redistribution is also achieved through regulating the capital market by prohibiting usury. The absence of a market rate of interest will obviously be a disincentive to lending but the law deals with this too: 'If there be among you a poor man of one of thy brethren within any of thy gates . . . thou shalt not harden thine heart nor shut thine hand from thy poor brother: But thou shalt . . . surely lend him sufficient for his need, in that which he wanteth' (Deut. 15:7-8). Collateral is something purely nominal: clothes given as a pledge must be returned at night in case that is the person's only possession.

Apart from having a direct effect on the redistribution of income and wealth, the regulation of the capital market would also have slowed down the rate of economic growth and indirectly prevented large accumulation of capital by individual families. The accumulation of wealth would be also prevented by other restrictions; once the Sabbatical year has arrived there is no moral responsibility to repay the loan. Work could only be substituted for leisure to a limited extent because of the strict prohibition against work on the Sabbath; and most of all by the principle of jubilee. On each jubilee year all land would be returned to its original owner. The description of jubilee starts with these words: 'The land shall not be sold for ever: for the land is mine' (Lev. 25:23). On the year of jubilee all slaves are freed, all debts are cancelled and the land lies fallow. Interestingly there is no evidence that this ever happened, so it is considered by de Vaux as 'a Utopian law'.[5] Nevertheless it is a critical part of the ideal of the Jewish economic system.

Lastly, in the Old Testament wealth is seen as the blessing of God. 'Thou shalt remember the Lord thy God: for it is he that giveth thee power to get wealth, that he may establish his covenant which he sware unto thy fathers' (Deut. 8:18).

The economic system of the Old Testament is by modern standards a curious mixture: a strong emphasis on private property rights circumscribed by certain laws; a simple welfare system and income redistribution mechanisms, some fiscal, others not; and restrictions on the accumulation of capital. The major objectives of this system were to guarantee the individual a measure of economic security and to ensure that each family was not permanently debarred from participating in the economic life of the nation through temporary misfortune. One thing I have always found with this system is the difficulty of classifying it as either capitalism or socialism. One particular aspect of the economic life of Israel which has received great attention in the history of the Church and which needs further expansion is the prohibition on usury. Strictly defined usury is the payment of interest for the borrowing and lending of money. It is not the payment of interest at exorbitant rates and so we are not dealing necessarily with a monopoly situation. Usury was forbidden among Jews but was not forbidden in loans made by Jews to foreigners. 'Do not demand interest on loans you make to a brother Israelite. Whether it is in the form of money, food or anything else. You may take interest from a foreigner but not from a fellow Jew' (Deut. 23:9-20). In assessing this particular restriction two points need to be made. First, usury is not intrinsically wrong in the way that murder, adultery or theft are wrong. If usury was wrong in itself then the Israelites would have been prohibited from charging interest on any funds lent, not just funds lent to fellow Jews. Second, it is important to consider the circumstances of the borrower. Borrowing at this time was not the kind of consumer or investment borrowing which we so frequently observe today. It was undertaken generally by people who had experienced personal misfortune. Individual farmers had come across difficult times and they needed to borrow to finance seed to plant for the next year's crop. As a result debt is described in the Pentateuch as a form of slavery. At the same time there was no organised capital market and so interest rates might be high. We do not know what interest rates were in Israel but we do know that the annual rate of interest in the ancient Near East was very high: in Babylonia and Assyria it was 20–25 per cent for money loans, 33 per cent for loans in kind and frequently more; in Upper Mesopotamia and Elam rates were higher, reaching 50 per cent for money loans; in the Ptolemaic period in Egypt rates seem to have been around 12 per cent.[6] The prohibition of usury in the Old Testament, therefore, should not be taken as criticism of a modern competitive capital market. It was never an absolute prohibition and its main justification was as a form of consumer protection in view of the position of the borrowers and the local nature of the market.

The Coming of the Kingdom and the Teaching of Jesus

The third element in a Biblical view is the life and teaching of Jesus. To understand his teaching on economic issues and how it relates to the Old Testament we need to understand the emphasis which he placed on the Kingdom of God. The Kingdom of God was central to his mission, the expression occurring over one hundred times in the Gospels. For example, both Matthew and Mark record that at the start of His ministry Jesus 'went about . . . preaching the gospel of the Kingdom, healing every disease . . . ' (Mt. 4:23, Mk 1:34) When he was about to commission his twelve disciples, he said, 'Go to the lost sheep of the house of Israel, and preach as you go, saying "the Kingdom of Heaven is near" '. (Mt. 10:5-7) He used similar words when he appointed the Seventy.

The idea of a political kingdom was something as easily understood then as now: a territory ruled over by a king to whom its citizens are subject. Using this analogy Jesus described his own mission in terms of establishing a Kingdom. The

Kingdom of God means the reign of Jesus Christ over those people who acknowledge him as Lord. The establishment of this Kingdom is described as good news, liberation and salvation. Jesus went about healing diseases, raising the dead, casting out demons. The religious establishment of his day once asked him, 'By what authority do you cast out demons?' and he replied, 'If it is by the finger of God that I cast out demons, then the Kingdom of God has come upon you.' In the Gospels the Kingdom of God is invariably associated with the presence of Christ and evidence of supernatural justice. He told various parables to illustrate what the Kingdom of God is like: it is like a person discovering treasure in a field, so he sells everything he has and buys the field; or like finding an extremely expensive piece of jewellery.

The New Testament teaches us that God is present and active in this world through his Holy Spirit, who is able to enter the hearts of individuals, giving new qualities of life and understanding in a way which we cannot fully grasp, though we can experience it. This is a miraculous and supernatural act of God.

As subjects of the King we are to obey his laws, and his laws are spelt out in the Sermon on the Mount. They involve a life of self-denial and sacrifice. Jesus put it in these words, 'If any man would come after me, let him deny himself and take up his cross daily and follow me.'

God is establishing a Kingdom, therefore, into which he is calling people from every country, race and class. The one thing its citizens have in common is that God has come into the life of each one and given a love for him and for each other which no human or political institution can ever produce.

When Jesus was on trial, he was asked by Pilate, 'Are you a king?' Jesus replied in those intriguing words, 'My kingdom is not of this world.' In answering this question he was contrasting his own Kingdom with an earthly kingdom. The origin of his Kingdom was not in succession, nor as the result of conquest, expansion or power. The weapons of his Kingdom were not those normally used by political rulers. One of the greatest temptations Jesus ever faced was when the devil said to him,

'Here are the Kingdoms of the world; they can be yours if you worship me.' The Establishment of Jesus's day would have liked him to establish a political kingdom for the Jews, but he said, 'My kingdom is not of this world.'

It is against this that we must judge Jesus's teaching on economic matters. Nowhere in the teaching of Jesus is there a systematic statement on this subject. Jesus was not a social reformer with a social message who produced a socio-economic blueprint for society. His primary purpose was to announce and establish the Kingdom of God and in calling people to follow him to put material matters in their true perspective. His followers are to trust in the goodness and providence of their heavenly father and abandon their care about the material world. They are to store up treasure in heaven and not on earth. The service of God is incompatible with the service of Mammon. Against the background of a Judaism in which even the Pharisees had become thoroughly materialistic, Jesus's primary message in this whole area is of the danger of materialism.

This criticism of materialism is seen in all his teaching. The successful farmer (Luke 12) who is eager to expand his business is censured by our Lord not because of his wealth or success but because of his exclusive concern with himself, his own happiness and his wealth. In the story of the rich man and Lazarus, the rich man's wealth insulates him from the poverty and the suffering of Lazarus. In the parable of the sower the thorns which choke the growing seed so making it barren are the "worldly cares and the false glamour of wealth" (Matt. 13). The attractive rich young Jewish politician who wished to follow Jesus was instructed by our Lord to sell his wealth. In doing this Jesus pinpointed the one thing in his life which he was not prepared to renounce to follow him. And he followed it up by that shrewd observation "It is easier for a camel to go through the eye of a needle than for a rich man to enter the kingdom of God' (Mark 10:25). Our Lord is teaching in these parables and encounters that the pursuit of wealth can so easily become an obstacle to entering the Kingdom. Why? Because wealth breeds arrogance, self-satisfaction, smugness and an indifference and carelessness to the needs of others.

But nowhere in his teaching does Jesus condemn wealth as such. In none of his parables or stories or recorded interviews does he ever suggest that the material world is evil and that wealth is in itself bad. For him to have done this he would have had to deny the teaching of the Old Testament. In his family background and dealings with people there is no suggestion that the material world is intrinsically evil. His home was not that of a day labourer or landless tenant but that of a middle-class artisan. Joseph was most probably a mason, carpenter, cartwright and joiner. Jesus took the ownership of private property for granted. He visited the home of Simon Peter, was supported by well-to-do people and never encouraged Zacchaeus to dispose of the whole of his wealth at the time when he returned money to those he had cheated. In the parable of the unjust steward, our Lord applauds the cleverness, astuteness and prudence of the unjust steward and in conclusion addresses his listeners, 'Use your worldly wealth to win friends for yourselves so that when money is a thing of the past you may be received into an eternal home' (Luke 16:9). The injunction which still holds good is that we should use our resources with as much single-mindedness and astuteness as the unjust steward displayed but in our case to further the interests of the Kingdom of God.

To summarise therefore, the teaching of Jesus on this subject is intimately bound up with his establishment of the Kingdom: it is not a condemnation of wealth as such but a much-needed perspective on the material world in an age of materialism. He develops at length the way in which the pursuit of wealth can numb spiritual realities but combines this with the injunction to exercise personal stewardship over those resources with which we have been entrusted.

The Life of the Early Church

In Acts we have two vivid descriptions of what has come to be called the communism of the early Church: 'All who believed were together and had all things in common; and they sold their possessions and goods and distributed them to all, as any had need' (Acts 2:44-5); and 'No one said that any of the things which he possessed was his own, but they had everything in common . . . There was not a needy person among them, for as many as were possessors of lands or houses sold them, and brought the proceeds of what was sold and laid it at the apostles' feet; and distribution was made to each as any had need' (Acts 4:32, 34-5).

What happened in the Jerusalem Church took place against the background of Pentecost — a time when the Holy Spirit was given in a remarkable way, so that in Jerusalem thousands believed and were baptised. It says of this charismatic community that they met constantly to pray, to break bread, to hear the apostles teach and to share their common life together. The form which their material sharing took involved two important features. First, it was spontaneous and not master-minded. Second, it was voluntary not compulsory. They were not instructed to do so by the apostles and their doing it was not a condition of membership of the church community. Some still retained private property as is evidenced by the fact that they met in private houses and that they would sell their assets if people were seen to be in need. Earnest Troeltsch is absolutely correct to describe it as a love communism.

It forms an interesting contrast to both the contemporary communities of the Essenes and to current Marxist ideas. The Essenes were a monastic order (Josephus suggests they originated around 150 BC) whose aim was complete separation from the world in order to live a life of holiness and total devotion to God. At the time of Pentecost they appear to have numbered around four thousand (dependent on Josephus, Philo and Pliny) and to have established communities in most of the villages of Palestine. Each community was organised independently, with membership by initiation into secret rites, and then after three years full membership being conferred. Although independent they were linked to each other. What is important however is that they practised a strict form of communism. All property was communally owned and each person was required to give all his assets including clothes to the community. They were engaged in agriculture and industry but they renounced trade. They gave up every kind of luxury and frequently bathed in cold water. There were also elements of non-Judaistic thinking in their practice of sun worship. As far as the sharing and common ownership of property is concerned what is important is to notice the contrast between the communism of the Acts which was spontaneous and voluntary and that of the Essenes which was strictly organised and fixed by law.

The communism of the early Church is also an interesting contrast to Marxist egalitarianism. The essential feature of the community of Jerusalem Christians was their total other-worldliness, i.e. the three-key decision (a) between work and leisure; (b) between consumption, saving and giving; and (c) between accumulating and selling assets was not to be influenced by personal consumption and gain. In other words communism under freedom is possible only to the extent that people are motivated by non-economic rewards. Marxism in practice however is not voluntary but forced, not spontaneous but planned. Equality is possible only when people are systematically denied the freedom to choose.

What can be concluded? In the early Church common ownership is only practised at Jerusalem and not at other churches. It is not even mandatory for Christians there, simply a description of what happened. There is no suggestion even in the passage quoted earlier from the Acts that as Christians we should strive for communism and equality — rather our concern within the church community should be a genuine caring for those in need. That is fundamental and should influence our Churches. But to attempt to implement such principles in society as a whole will be disastrous unless people are seriously interested in material reward.

Eschatology

The fifth key Biblical element is Eschatology. The Christian

90

faith is a view of history; a process which not only has a beginning in creation but an end signalled by the personal return of Jesus Christ and the establishment of 'a new heavens and a new earth'. St Paul expresses this fact by saying that 'the created universe waits with eager expectation for God's sons to be revealed. It was made the victim of frustration . . . but is to be freed from the shackles of mortality and enter upon the liberty and splendour of the children of God.' (Rom 8) Not only are there the promises of Jesus himself on which to base this expectation but there is the evidence of the resurrection. That was a victory in history over the power of sin and death. If our Lord had been resurrected only as a spirit it would have signified a victory over the spiritual world but the fact that it was a physical resurrection shows his sovereignty over history and the created world. For the Christian, therefore, history is not an unknown adventure, but a process which will end with the reign of Christ and the establishment of a just society. The goal of history for the Christian is therefore the restitution of all things.

Christian Guidelines for Economic Life

Having outlined the key elements in a Biblical view of economic life, the next question is how are these put together? How do we attempt to deduce some general guidelines from his history and teaching which are of relevance for us today? I believe that this is a critical question. We start from the Biblical revelation, having a high regard for the text. We want to address ourselves to concrete problems in today's world. In attempting to do this, the intermediate step by which we attempt to develop certain guidelines is crucial. Incidentally it is just at this point that I find many theologians who enter this field particularly weak; mainly because what they deduce from a Biblical view is so general (and sometimes even vague) that it is of little practical help in choosing between the main alternatives of the world today. I would like to emphasise the following guidelines:

First, there is a positive mandate to create wealth. The

Christian has a distinctive view of the physical world. It is neither sacred nor magic. It is God's intention that we cultivate it, improve it and harness its resources for our own use. Man has been created to have dominion in this world. The urge to control, direct and manage the resources of this world is part and parcel of man's nature and vocation. Idleness is at root alien to human personality. It was never part of God's intention that poverty should be the norm for economic life. Prosperity, not poverty, is God's intention for his world, though we must be careful to distinguish prosperity from luxury. In the Bible, therefore, economic life has a legitimacy which derives from the nature of the created world. There is nothing inherently grubby, dirty or second rate about the whole business of getting and spending. This positive mandate to create wealth however is in the context of our fiduciary responsibilities. This world is God's world not ours. We are invested with the responsibilities of trusteeship. We are not free to deface and destroy the natural world. We are accountable to the Creator. In this as in other areas the ends can never justify the means. The order to create wealth can never justify permanent damage to the balance of nature.

Second, private property rather than state, social or collective ownership is the Christian norm for society. God alone has total and unconditional ownership of property. 'The absolute and transcendental title to property is the Lord's; the present and historical title to property is man's.' Throughout the Bible private property is the normal and accepted form of ownership and there is no conflict between trusteeship and private property rights. This was the form of property rights used when the land was parcelled out among families in Israel. Even though the idea of community was so strong in the Pentateuch and even though society was organised along tribal lines, it is important to notice that property rights were not communal, they were private. This was not accidental. The justification of private property rights in a Judaeo-Christian world-view is rooted in creation. Man was created as a responsible being. But freedom presupposes the ability to make choices concerning those things over which persons have control. In the material area of life this can be guaranteed only by the existence of private property rights. As a result, in the Eighth Commandment, God protects private property. 'Thou shalt not steal.' Emil Brunner, the Swiss theologian, argues the case forcefully as follows:

> The man who has nothing at his disposal cannot act freely. He is dependent on the permission of others for every step he takes, and if they so wish they can make it impossible for him to carry on any concrete activity. Without property there is no free personal life. Without property there is no power to act . . . And the word 'property' must be taken literally as ownership or, as we say today, private property. Without private property there is no freedom. [7]

Contrast this with a Marxist view of property rights. The logic of the Marxist argument is as follows: men are created equal; private property is theft; such injustice can only be removed by state ownership. But an economic system without the freedom established by property rights results in the direction of labour and capital — something described so powerfully by Solzhenitsyn as the Gulag Archipelago. A hundred years ago Professor Charles Hodge, a Princeton theologian, put it very clearly in his systematic theology:

> The foundation of the right to property is the will of God . . . This doctrine of the divine right of property is the only security for the individual or for society. If it be made to rest on any other foundation it is insecure and unstable. It is only by making property sacred, guarded by the fiery sword of divine justice that it can be safe from the dangers to which it is everywhere and always exposed. [8]

This is precisely what the Eighth Commandment does when it says 'Thou shalt not steal'.

I believe that when Milton Friedman defends capitalism as a necessary but not sufficient condition to ensure a free society, it is not capitalism as an ideology to which he refers, but the guarantee by the state to respect private property rights.

But one thing needs to be made clear. The Christian view of private property rights is different from the Roman or Justinian view which derived ownership from the concept of natural right. In a Roman view ownership meant the unconditional and exclusive use of property by the individual. He was free to choose (subject of course to the law of contract) exactly how he wished to use that property. By contrast a Judaeo-Christian view places emphasis on duties as well as rights — think of the poor-tithe, the gleaning laws and the legislation of a zero rate of interest in the Pentateuch economy.

Third, each family should have a permanent stake in economic life. The basic unit for society is and always has been the family. Because of this the Judaeo-Christian world-view recognises the need to create political and economic structures which ensure that the family is not debarred from a permanent interest in economic life. In a simple agricultural community, such as that at the time of the Pentateuch, this meant each family being able to own land. The principle which underlay the concept of Jubilee, (that all land alienated during the preceeding fifty years was to be returned to its original owner or his descendants) was that each family should not find itself in a position in which it was permanently barred from owning land, the vital productive asset in that economy. As a result of industrialisation land has been replaced by capital as the most important means of production and in the process, real wages or, expressed differently the value of human capital, has increased as well. In my judgment therefore the equivalent of this principle today is the right of each family to home ownership, the need for more diffused and direct ownership of equity capital and the opportunity not just for a formal education but for retraining and post-experience training in later life.

There is also the other side to this particular coin. In the Judaeo-Christian view, while the state has the responsibility for ensuring that the family is an on-going economic concern, the family has the responsibility to look after itself and the welfare of its members.

Fourth, the relief and elimination of poverty rather than the pursuit of economic equality should be a Christian concern. The concept of equality has dominated the twentieth century. The Bible teaches clearly that all men are created equal in the sight of God. God knows, values and loves each one of his creatures. The American Declaration of Independence declared as self-evident truths 'that all men are created equal, that they are endowed by the Creator with certain inalienable Rights: that among these are Life, Liberty and the pursuit of Happiness'. The recognition that all men are equal in the sight of God is fundamental to liberty as we know it in modern Western societies. Equality before God leads of necessity to equality before the law. It is an essential characteristic of a Christian society. By the seventh and eighth centuries BC Israel had become quite wealthy. Alongside wealth had come materialism and with it injustice, the oppression of the poor, bribery and corruption and the abuse of the legal system by the wealthy — with one law for the rich and another for the poor. Such inequality was roundly condemned by the Old Testament prophets.

But there is all the difference in the world between people created as equal before God, having equal access to the law, and the way in which equality is used so frequently today: not as equality of opportunity but as equality of outcome. Economic justice, so it is claimed, demands economic equality — defined as an equalised after-tax real income. But this concept is quite alien to Scripture. As we saw earlier there were various mechanisms built into the Hebrew economic system to prevent permanent and substantial economic inequality from developing. But there is never a suggestion in Scripture that economic justice implies economic equality. Indeed as we have seen economic equality in society could only be achieved under two kinds of circumstances — *one* through the use of coercion in which case it is incompatible with freedom and the *other* in a situation in which people do not respond or even care about material rewards.

The authentic Christian concern is not in creating equality but in relieving poverty. Three major causes of poverty can be distinguished in the Bible: *first,* oppression and exploitation — the typical situation being that of an employer using monopoly power or the use of fraud and violence in order to pay low wages; *second,* misfortune, such as the position of widows, orphans, or as a result of accident and injury; *third,* laziness. In the first case the appropriate response is to remove the cause of the poverty; in the second to meet the needs of those who are deprived; and in the third to do nothing. The Old Testament however is not just a clinical analysis of poverty. When God instructs his people Israel to care for the poor, the appeal is invariably on the basis of what he has done for them.

> You shall not wrong a stranger or oppress him, for you were strangers in the land of Egypt. You shall not afflict any widow or orphan. If you do afflict them, and they cry out to me, I will surely hear their cry; and my wrath will burn, and I will kill you with the sword, and your wives shall become widows and your children fatherless — (Exod. 22:21-4).

Fifth, economic injustice is to be remedied. In Biblical times injustice resulted from the exploitation of monopoly power in grain, corn, food and in the employment of labour. Injustice in this sense is not measured by the level of wages but the extent of oppression, exploitation, cheating and forced labour: something all too familiar in the early stages of industrialisation in the UK and in certain American countries today, not to mention the labour camps of the Soviet Union.

Listen to the prophetic note throughout Scripture:

Jer. 22:13-17   'And woe to you, King Jehoiakim, for you are building your great palace with forced labour. By not paying wages you are building injustice into its walls and oppression into the doorframes and ceilings.

'Why did your father Josiah reign so long? Because he was just and fair in all his dealing that is why God blessed him. He saw to it that justice and help were given to the poor and the needy and all went well for him. This is how a man lives close to God. But you! You are full of selfish greed and all dishonesty! You murder the innocent, oppress the poor and reign with ruthlessness.'

Lev. 19:13 'You shall not rob nor oppress anyone and you shall pay your hired workers promptly. If something is due to them, don't even keep it overnight.'

James 5:4 'Hear the cries of the field workers whom you have cheated of their pay'.

Malachi 3:5 'At that time my punishments will be quick and certain: I will move swiftly against wicked men who trick the innocent, against adulteress, and liars, against all those who cheat their hired hands or oppress widows and orphans, or defraud strangers and do not fear me'.

Apart from condemning the abuse of economic power, the Bible has little to say in a positive sense as to what constitutes fair and just wages and prices. The notion of what constitutes a just wage and a just price has in consequence been a much debated question in the history of the Church. In my judgment it is difficult to improve on a genuinely competitive wage or price. That is, most of the grounds of injustice in this area stem from the presence of monopoly power and the disregard of a law. I find it difficult to believe that we can improve on trying to establish competitive markets within the framework of a rule of law.

Sixth, there is the constant warning of materialism. Money, wealth and profit have a legitimacy in a Christian world-view: but they also carry a danger. The Tenth Commandment, 'Thou shalt not covet thy neighbour's house', recognises that the quite legitimate desire for prosperity and ownership may be misdirected. Instead of being an act of service, making money and owning things can become purely selfish activities; and it is in this sense that our Lord issues the warning that 'you cannot

97

serve both God and Mammon, and tells the story of the very prosperous farmer who is destroyed by his self-indulgence. In an age which has become dominated by the Gross National Product and the Dow–Jones Index, the level of interest rates and the state of the pound, the money supply and the Public Sector Deficit, and at a more mundane level, the Sunday colour supplements offering a world of gourmet food and package holidays in the sun, it is a warning which is easily muffled by our culture.

Seventh, accountability and judgment are an integral part of economic life. The Christian has a high view of man. Although part of nature in that he is made from dust, he is nevertheless created in the image of God and as such possesses many of the qualities of Godhead: mind, will, emotions, conscience. He is the supreme achievement of God's creation. Yet despite this he is created in a relationship of accountability to God and the sphere of his accountability includes the economic. He is accountable as a steward of the earth's resources; he is accountable for his own particular talents; and he is accountable for the way in which he acquires and disposes of his wealth.

It is within this context that we have to come to terms with the Christian view of judgment which is arguably the most unfashionable Biblical doctrine of the twentieth century. Judgment is frequently thought of in a retributive and future context. It is the verdict passed on those who choose self rather than God. An unprejudiced reading of the New Testament certainly suggests that to be true. The successful farmer of Luke and the story of the rich man and Lazarus are sufficient evidence of that. But judgment can be present as well as future. The process of sowing and reaping is evidenced now. Actions have consequences. Throughout the Old Testament God actively judges people and nations. In this context we may well ask whether we are not living in an age when God is judging our Western civilisation — whether the inflation of the Western world is a judgment on materialism, or the rising unemployment a judgment on militant trade unionism or the crisis of capitalism a judgment on the secular humanism of our age.

So far, we have considered some key principles derivative from a Christian world-view which are relevant to issues of political economy. But in conclusion I should like to emphasise that Christianity places emphasis not only on structures but also on personal obedience. The structures of the Pentateuch were good but a stable and wealthy economic society could only flourish to the extent that Israel was obedient to the whole of the law and its commandment. In this sense a set of Christian guidelines must never be interpreted as an attempt to legislate the Gospel. Proper structures are desirable in themselves but by themselves they are never a substitute for that vital Christian life which comes from personal commitment to follow Jesus Christ. The New Testament has a good deal to say with respect to church administration. But a Biblically constituted Church is no guarantee that it will be a community of life, growth and love. Similarly, just economic structures are I believe a part of God's intention for human society. But we must never forget that the good news of the Incarnation is that God's supreme revelation is of personal liberation which we can all experience in Jesus Christ which in turn will help to shape and mould those structures which we have considered.

CHAPTER 4

REFORMING THE MARKET ECONOMY

What is interesting about Christian guidelines for economic life is that they cannot easily be classified as either right wing or left wing, capitalist or socialist. They do not fit in readily with any contemporary ideology or with the manifesto of any established political party. In terms of the present debate between capitalism and socialism, they are fundamentally different from the prescriptions of both Karl Marx and Milton Friedman. A Christian approach to economic life could be described in various ways. I would summarise it myself in terms of a market economy bounded by Christian principles of justice. To the extent that private property rights rather than state ownership are the appropriate Christian starting point, then a market economy rather than a soviet-style state is the logical outcome. After all, a market is simply a place in which property rights are exchaged. In a Christian world-view therefore the superiority of the market over a state-owned economy is based on a comparison not of the efficiency but of the humanity of the two systems.

In this chapter, I would like to examine the relevance of these guidelines for the direction in which we should be seeking to reform the basic economic institutions of the UK economy. Before I do so I must say something about the way in which the UK economy has developed since the latter half of the nineteenth century.

The Corporatist Welfare State and the Crisis of Humanism

The contrast between the British economy at the end of the nineteenth century and at the present is quite striking. In the late nineteenth century the UK dominated the international economy and London was the centre of the world's financial system. Sterling was linked to gold and the gold standard ensured price stability. Fiscal policy was conservative. The Gladstonian principle that public sector budgets should be balanced — increased expenditure met by increased taxes — was the accepted rule. Government participation in economic life was relatively small – the percentage of GNP taken by the government at the turn of the century being less than 10 per cent; and the creation of wealth was carried out very largely by private enterprise. The state was concerned with the alleviation of poverty but its direct participation in welfare programmes was small; most of this was left to private charity. Trade unions had been growing throughout the nineteenth century but they were still without those distinctive legal privileges which they acquired in 1906. In terms of the international economy, free trade was the order of the day.

Today the British economy is best described as a corporate welfare state. In economic terms the state has now become a mammoth corporation which produces coal, steel, oil, gas and electricity; the primary source of rail and major source of air and other transport services; the greatest property and house owner in the whole country; a provider of most educational and health services; a massive supplier of welfare services, for the young, the old, the pregnant, the unemployed, the disabled and the poor; and a disposer of grants and subsidies on a scale hitherto unknown in human societies. In Orwellian terms it is indeed the Ministry of Plenty. As a response to events and ideas, economic life has become increasingly politicised and the workings of a modern mixed economy effected by a social contract between government, the corporate sector and the trade unions. It is questionable whether the real centre of economic power in this country is any longer an elected parliament or whether it has moved to the trade unions, large corporations, government departments, nationalised industries and government agencies. The activities of private companies have become controlled increasingly through government-sponsored economic and social policy in such fields as price control, the quality of the product, health and safety legislation and employment protection. At the same time, the rules which guided fiscal and monetary policy in Gladstonian Britain have been abandoned in favour of activist and discretionary policies in which governments attempt to manipulate total spending to provide full employment, property and stability. The most noticeable feature of the past few decades however, has been the increasing instability of economic life. Over the decades of the sixties and seventies, when the role of government in economic life grew rapidly, we have witnessed a high but uneven rate of inflation, unstable interest rates and exchange rates, declining productivity growth and a rising trend rate of unemployment.

The emergence of such a system is a response to both events and ideas. To start with there was in the late nineteenth century the growth of America and Germany as industrial powers, having a comparative advantage in the production of commodities such as iron, steel and chemicals which had until then been the preserve of the UK. Obviously this necessitated change in the industrial structure of this country. Rather than face up to change, however, politicians, especially in the Conservative Party, campaigned for the use of the tariff to keep out foreign goods and to provide subsidies to British industry and so slow down the process of adjustment.

The second major event to shape economic life in this country was the depression of the twenties and the thirties. This increased the demand for protectionism and throughout the postwar years British industry was sheltered from foreign competition by higher tariffs, import quotas and exchange controls. At the same time the severity of the recession led to demands for much greater state intervention in industry. The result was the rationalisation of the industrial structure, which Professor G.C. Allen has summed up: 'The chief effect of government intervention between the wars was to defend the failures rather than to encourage the enterprising'.[1] The recession also led to the demand for the provision of greater economic security for the average citizen, which became embodied subsequently in the growth of the welfare state following the election of the Labour Government in 1945. In the world of economic theory the Great Depression had one very important effect. It led to the publication in 1936 of *The General Theory of Interest, Employment and Money* by J.M. Keynes, a Cambridge don, which revolutionised conventional economics and which resulted in a new approach to the conduct of economic policy. Keynes argued that the slump was the result of deficient demand, and that the level of unemployment could only be remedied by increased government expediture, financed by the printing and sale of government bonds. After the Second World War successive governments conducted economic policies along Keynesian lines in order to achieve full employment. Another major event which has affected the British economy is the decline of the British Empire and Commonwealth, linked as it was in a major way to the two world wars of this century. It would be difficult to substantiate Lenin's theory of imperialism as applied to the British Empire. The evidence suggests that Britain paid the world price for raw materials bought from these countries. However, the First World War resulted in a loss of markets, especially in India and Latin America and the Second World War resulted in a sale of foreign assets and the abolition of imperial preferences as a condition for the lend-lease agreement with the US to finance the war.

In the realm of ideas, there were many influences throughout the period but I would like to single out three in particular. One powerful assault on the private enterprise system came from people such as Thomas Arnold, a headmaster of Rugby School, and his son Matthew Arnold, from John Ruskin and Thomas Carlyle. Thomas Arnold made a great deal out of the distinction between the concept of service and the pursuit of profit. For him service was the Christian ideal which underlay the professions. It involved the acceptance of a vocation to be undertaken not for money but from a sense of duty. As a result we still refer to the civil service, military service, social service, health service, library service and so on. By contrast, industry and commerce was concerned with profit and the amassing of personal

103

fortune. Matthew Arnold was even more critical of the system than his father. In *Culture and Anarchy* he divided society into three classes: the barbarians (the aristocracy), the philistines (the emerging middle class based on the newly created industrial wealth) and the populace. To Arnold the term philistine implied the idea of something stiff-necked and perverse in its resistance to light – 'and therein it specially suits our middle class, who not only do not pursue sweetness and light, but who even prefer to them that sort of machinery of business, chapels, tea-meetings and addresses from Mr Murphy, which makes up the dismal and illiberal life on which I have so oftened touched'.[2]

In a chapter of the book entitled Hebraism and Hellenism he traces the roots of these views. The governing idea of Hellenism is spontaneity of consciousness while that of Hebraism is strictness of conscience, the former concerned with intelligence, thinking and knowing the ground of one's duty, the latter with obedience, doing and the diligent practice of one's duty. He was quite explicit in rejecting the world of business because of its philistinism, derived from a Judaistic view of the world, and championing a Hellenistic view concerned with the pursuit of sweetness and light. But ideas have consequences. The emphasis on service linked to the pursuit of beauty and truth led in the British educational system to the superiority of pure over applied science and technology, and the superiority of classics and humanities over more vocational subjects. It meant that business was devalued relative to the professions so that even now a career in business ranks second in the minds of many new graduates to a career in one of the more established professions.

A second powerful assault on the system came from the concept of egalitarianism, which had several roots — the Webbs and the Fabian Society, Bentham and the utilitarians and Karl Marx. Equality has been a powerful theme in British politics since the turn of the century and can be seen in practice in the high marginal rates of income tax in the postwar years reaching until recently a marginal tax of 83 per cent on earned income and 98 per cent on unearned income; the drive to abolish private education and private health; the 'euthanasia of the rentier' through rent control; and the provision of state welfare services financed by taxation but free of charge at the time they are used.

Linked to egalitarianism and associated with many of the same writers and thinkers has been the drift to collectivism. If society perceives something to be a problem the solution is provided by government. Unlike consumers and corporations who have clearly defined self-interests, the state is considered an impartial body, acting in the public interest and free from any of the narrow objectives pursued, it is alleged, by the business community in particular. And so the incredible growth of government throughout this century has been in response to all kinds of problems: economic insecurity, unemployment, declining industries, poverty, natural monopolies, external costs, pollution, inflation. Unlike North America the involvement of government in economic life has been through the increased regulation of the private sector; in the UK it has resulted in the public ownership of the industries or utilities concerned. The dominant values of the past century therefore have cast doubt on the value of creating wealth and placed much greater emphasis on its redistribution. They have produced a decline of the market economy and increasing government involvement in industrial life.

Another area of changed values which has had important effects is the growth of the concept of freedom and the decline in the importance of rules. Controlling the money supply in Victorian Britain was technically quite easy because of adherence to a gold standard. But why did society voluntarily accept the constraints imposed by the gold standard? It was partly because of the dominant part played by the Christian religion in that society, with its emphasis on the importance of adherence to rules as the basis for personal conduct and the need for absolute standards in the life of society. Although there was a technical dimension to the economic stability of Victorian Britain its roots were firmly moral and religious. Gladstone's case for a balanced budget was above all a moral not a technical one. 'An excess in the public expenditure beyond the legitimate wants of the country is not only a pecuniary waste but a great political and above all, a great moral evil.'

By contrast, we live in a society which has largely abandoned rules, both personally and collectively. The one word which sums up our society is freedom. In this respect no figure is more characteristic of the twentieth century than the highly influential economist John Maynard Keynes. Late in his life, summing up the views of his Bloomsbury friends and himself, he put it like this:

> We entirely repudiated a personal liability on us to obey general rules. We claimed the right to judge every individual case on its merits, and the wisdom, experience and self-control to do so successfully. We repudiated entirely customary morals, conventions and traditional wisdom. We were, that is to say, in the strict sense of the term immoralists . . . we recognised no moral obligation, no inner sanction, to confirm or obey . . . So far as I am concerned, it is too late to change. I remain and always will remain an immoralist.[3]

It would be impertinent to suggest that Keynes dichotomised his private and professional life and in this sense discretionary monetary policy and deficit spending by government although recommended as a technical solution to a technical problem, must be seen as the prescriptions of a self-confessed immoralist.

It is important to notice that in terms of ideas, the major influences on the British economy for the last hundred years have all been thoroughly secular — Matthew Arnold's Hellenism, the Webbs' egalitarianism and Keynes's immoralism. This is not to say of course, that Christians might not have supported certain of these ideas: by choosing a particular profession of considerable sacrifice to themselves in economic terms, by supporting rent legislation because of the plight of deprived families, by welcoming the welfare state because of the inability of poor families to obtain appropriate medical treatment or by applauding deficit spending as a way of reducing unemployment. However good the intentions it is

106

possible in retrospect to see that the drift towards the modern corporatist welfare state has been dominated by secular humanism. The prevailing ethos today is that the state not the individual is responsible for his welfare, that the erosion of private property rights and the control by the state of many areas of our lives is legitimate and welcome and that the distribution of wealth must take precedence over its creation. However well-intentioned an Arnold or an Attlee or a Keynes or a Webb I suspect that the outcome can hardly be what they envisaged.

DISSECTING THE CORPORATE STATE

In view of the fact that the growth of the modern corporate welfare state has been a response to the rise of secular humanism, it is important to go one step further and analyse in greater depth the three key elements within the corporate state — private companies, government and trade unions.

CORPORATIONS

Private corporations are still the major institutions responsible for the creation of wealth in the Western world and the modern corporation is very much an invention of the nineteenth century. From a legal point of view, the corporation is a person separate and distinct from its members yet joined to them by rights and duties. At the same time it is a business fund (joint stock) which again is separate and distinct from its subscribers, yet joined to them through debits and credits. In addition both of these are linked to an organisation administered by management and offering contractual employment. The major reason for limited liability was not the desire of business firms to expand but the need to find relatively safe investments for the funds of small savers. Unlike partnerships in which the partners decide policy, in the business corporation the equity owners relinquished their privilege in favour of the directors. As a result of this various safeguards were provided. *First,* the limited liability company had a constitution which stipulated an executive board of directors, their relationship to shareholders and the necessary meetings, elections and voting systems. *Second,* there was statutory requirement of disclosure, relating to constitutional documents, the names of directors and the disclosure of capital and accounts. And *third,* there was the prospect that in every area of manufacturing, trade and commerce new limited liability companies could be established which would keep existing companies on their toes. Since the mid-nineteenth century, the continuing reform of company law has tried to strike a balance between all of those parties which have an interest in the corporation — shareholders, creditors, directors, customers, suppliers and employees. In addition since that time a host of legislation has been passed separate from the companies acts which provides rights for each of the parties involved.

Nevertheless corporations continue to remain an object of criticism. One line of attack is the growth in the size of corporations. Professor S.J. Prais estimates that in 1909 the share of the hundred largest enterprises in manufacturing net output in the UK amounted to 16 per cent approximately, but by 1970 it had reached 40–41 per cent; while in the US over the same period the figure grew from 22 per cent to 33 per cent. In the UK most of this growth has occurred since 1950. At the same time the decline of the small manufacturing firm has been just as dramatic. Between 1930-68 the number of firms with 10 or less employees fell from 93,400 to 34,800. Another line of attack is that developed by A.A. Berle and G.C. Means in *The Modern Corporation and Private Property* published in 1932, namely the separation of ownership and control. While shareholders continue to retain the ownership of the corporation, control and in particular the design of corporate policy has passed to professional management. Even the reliance of companies on the stock market to raise finance is comparatively small. The recent Royal Commission on Incomes and Wealth analysed the sources of finance for the larger quoted industrial and financial companies in the UK and found that between 1950–72 internally generated funds accounted for an average 70 per cent of total finance over this period. The implication drawn from the trade is that modern corporations lack an adequate system of accountability. Examples which are typically given to support this view are the Distillers Co., Ltd, supplying the drug Thalidomide to the market without adequate tests, and investments in South Africa by many British companies. In addition there is the charge that the ownership of British companies has now passed to the large institutions — insurance companies, pension funds, unit trusts and investment trusts — who tend to adopt a rather passive approach to those companies whose equity they hold because they are more concerned with their own role as financial intermediaries.

However the modern corporation has also come under attack on grounds of Christian justice. First it is argued that the privilege granted to companies of limited liability violates the Christian concept of personal responsibility for one's actions. By limited liability the state is encouraging management to use shareholder funds in more risky ventures than they would otherwise undertake, and then pass on the liability at a time for forced liquidation, to third parties. In other words, limited liability is an incentive for management to play for high stakes and allow the general public to pick up the bill.

Arthur Bryant, the English historian, noted that

The consequences of the Companies Act of 1862 were perhaps greater than that of any single measure in English parliamentary history. They completed the divorce between the Christian conscience and the economic practice of everyday life. They paganised the commercial community. Henceforward an astute man by adherence to legal rules which had nothing to do with morality could grow immeasurably rich by virtue of shuffling off his most elementary obligations to his fellows. He could not only grow rich by these means. He could grow immensely rich.[4]

It is important to recognise that this criticism does have a certain validity. The modern corporation was founded on the principle of expediency. Limited liability is open to great abuse. However, in judging the framework of the modern corporation as an attempt to balance the interests, rights and responsibilities of all concerned it is important to take account of the welter of legislation, since the introduction of limited liability, which protects the interests of employees, consumers, suppliers and creditors. The history of company legislation over the past century can only be understood if it is seen as an attempt to rectify the imbalance and injustice resulting from the creation of limited liability in the mid-nineteenth century. The question facing us today is different. It is whether the pendulum has not swung too far in the other direction, so that the vitality, resourcefulness and dynamism of the modern corporation is sinking under the weight of excessive regulatory controls.

A second argument is that the system of property rights in which ownership and control are in the hands of shareholders violates the Christian concept of trusteeship and is contrary to the Biblical ideal of community. The modern corporation is seen as tantamount to a form of slavery because those who supply capital to the institution have almost total power, especially over employees. But from a Christian point of view, so it is argued, 'Providers of capital are merely owners of the capital goods . . . Their ownership right is a limited one which can never apply to the entire enterprise and the activities of its members.'[5] In this connection, it is interesting that many of the restrictions on economic life in the Pentateuch were to ensure that each family always had access to part of the society's capital — namely a plot of land and some animals. And also that the heart of Marx's critique of capitalism is that capital is owned by a professional class, the capitalists rather than those directly concerned with production, namely the workers.

GOVERNMENT

The growth of government in the twentieth century has been dramatic. The statistics speak for themselves. At the turn of the

110

century government expenditure as a proportion of GNP amounted to roughly 10 per cent; by 1970 this figure had reached over 40 per cent. The increase has not been at a constant rate. During the two world wars it rose very rapidly and then fell when peace was restored. Since 1960 it has risen very rapidly — by just over one third. As expenditure has risen so have taxes and the proportion of GNP taken up by taxes and social security payments is also around 40 per cent. In terms of current govenment spending, the most important item is social security, which accounts for just over a quarter of all public expenditure. The other major items are health, education and defence. Between them these items taken together account for 60 per cent of total expenditure. From a different point of view just under one third of the total of government spending is the wage bill of the public sector and an equivalent amount is current grants to persons.

The growth and size of government has had important economic and social consequences. As government grows, both individual freedom *and* individual responsibility are eroded. In order to pay for the growth in government, taxes have had to be raised. As a result in this country we have had a heavy tax burden and a structure of taxation which is a major disincentive to take risk, to invest and even to work. The growth and health of the black and informal economies is one clear evidence of the disincentive effects of taxation. At the same time the imbalance between expenditure and revenue has resulted in high interest rates and the deficit has been an engine driving inflation — as the monetisation of government debt is one cause of excessive money supply growth. But the growth of government has also been accompanied by a decline in the sense of individual responsibility: by parents for their children, by children for aging parents; by businessmen for the viability of their companies.

Something which is particularly curious is that increased government expenditure has not produced the egalitarian society which was intended. Tony Crosland, a great proponent of high public expenditure stated in a Fabian pamphlet:

We underestimated the capacity of the middle class to appropriate more than their fair share of public expenditure. They demand more resources for the school in their areas: they complain vociferously if they have to wait for their operations; they demand that the state intervene to subsidise the price of the rail tickets from their commuter homes to their work. Too often these pressures have been successful, and in consequence the distribution of public spending has been tilted away from the areas of greatest need, to those which generate the loudest demands.

It is the provision of welfare, however, which distinguishes the modern state from previous states.

It is clear that government has an important role to play in this area. In the Old Testament economy the poor tithe, the gleaning laws, the prohibition on usury were not options for the Jews. They were compulsory. The care for the poor was not to be undertaken by private charity as and when people decided to give but was to be organised by the society. It was a simple but effective system of welfare financed partly by taxes and partly by other devices. An individual who belonged to Israel had no choice with respect to paying the poor tithe. What is interesting about this system, however, is that it was a very limited system of welfare. It was selective and not general: it was determined by basic need and not simply as a way of reducing inequality. The poor were identified and compensated. It was not an indiscriminate method of handing out money to all and sundry. In the New Testament this is supplemented by the command that all Christians are to love their neighbours as themselves — an act of personal charity to those with whom we have contact. While the relief of poverty and personal compassion are imperative for the Christian there is a fundamental difference between a Christian view of relieving poverty and the whole thrust of the welfare state today. The modern welfare state is interested not so much in relieving poverty as redistributing income to achieve a more egalitarian distribution. Christians involved in the relief of poverty have been the first to point this out. Charles Booth in his classic study of *Life and Labour in London* puts the issue very clearly:

> The question of those who actually suffer from poverty should be considered separately from that of the true working classes, whose desire for a larger share of the wealth is of a different character. It is the plan of agitators and the way of sensational writers to confound the two in one, to talk of 'starving millions' and to tack on the thousands of the working classes to the tens or hundreds of the distressed. Against this method I protest. To confound these essentially distinct problems is to make the solution of both impossible. It is not by welding distress and aspiration that any good can be done.[6]

Professor Colin Clark, a modern distinguished economist, is equally unequivocal on this point.

> Most of our social services — let alone the construction of a Welfare State or 'Great Society' of universal welfare provision are morally valid. It is one thing to help those who are in special difficulties, or in real need. But when the state collects taxes in order to provide some of its citizens with services which they were capable of obtaining for themselves it is perpetrating a grave act of injustice on the taxpayers.

I believe that a Christian's position on this matter recognises the necessity for state action but goes on to argue that much of education, health and other welfare services could be quite adequately provided through the private sector, with the result that people would be free to exercise greater freedom of choice and also exercise greater responsibility over their lives.

TRADE UNIONS

The third element in the corporate state is the trade unions. Over the past few years I have read a great deal of specifically

113

Christian literature in the field of economics and I have been impressed by one thing: while much has been said about the immorality of the modern corporation and the injustice of the structures of international trade and while a little has been said, especially in North America, about the role of government and the need for proper control of money and credit, very little has been written about trade unions. Judged by existing Christian literature, it is almost as if trade unions hardly exist.

The origins of trade unions are to be found at the beginning of the nineteenth century and are a response to the rapid process of industrialisation and the change and dislocation which this caused. Even at that time, however, there was a difference between combinations and friendly societies — the one intent on using the collective power of the work force to make a change in real wages and the other developing a system of welfare services among members through cooperative effort. In view of everything that has happened since that time, this distinction is important. It also helps to explain the early opposition to combinations by members of the Clapham Sect. Even when this distinction is drawn, to the extent that the growth of trade unionism throughout the nineteenth century was a response to the power of local monopolies, unsafe working conditions, the use of physical violence by employees and the attempt to reduce the members of the work force to a situation of total dependency on the owners — a de facto form of slavery — then I believe that as Christians we should applaud the attempts of trade unionists to establish a more just and humane economic order.

Since that time, however, trade unions have grown in influence and power: at present more than 50 per cent of the British labour force is unionised. It is now widely believed that no British government is able to govern without the tacit support of the trade union movement.

Critical to the power which trade unions exercise in our society is their standing at law. The 1906 Trade Disputes Act granted trade unions total immunity for torts 'alleged to have been committed by or on behalf of the trade union'. A.V.

114

Dicey, the distinguished constitutional laywer, said of this that 'It makes a trade union a privileged body exempted from the ordinary law of the land. No such privileged body has ever before been deliberately created by an English Parliament.' Even Sidney and Beatrice Webb, in their classic history of trade unionism, said of the Act that it gave trade unions 'an extraordinary and unlimited immunity, however great may be the damage caused, and however unwarranted the act, which most lawyers as well as all employers, regard as nothing less than monstrous'.

Since that time successive attempts have been made to reform the position but to no avail. Following the General Strike in 1926, an act was passed in 1927 making political strikes illegal. It was repealed in 1946. In a judgment in 1964 the House of Lords in the case of Rooks v. Barnard found that a strike which was in breach of contract was illegal. In 1965 an Act was passed which reversed this judgment. In 1969 the Labour government under Harold Wilson produced a White Paper entitled *In Place of Strife*. Its major proposals were to give the Secretary of State for Employment the right to impose a twenty-eight day conciliation pause in the case of 'serious' unconstitutional strikes; the power to call a strike ballot of all members; and to establish a legal liability to certain financial penalties if trade union members failed to comply with such orders. The TUC was resolutely opposed to such measures and the proposals were withdrawn.

In 1971 the Industrial Relations Act was passed, which made trade union privileges conditional upon registering and satisfying the Registrar that their internal rules contained minimum safeguards for their members' rights. This Act was repealed by the new Labour government in 1974 and in legislation in 1975 and 1976, further rights and immunities were granted to trade unions. These Acts extended the powers of secondary picketing and the ability to negotiate closed shop agreements, and limited the grounds on which individuals could refuse to join a trade union.

In a judgment in the Court of Appeal (BBC v. Hearn and

others 1977) Lord Denning summed up the legal position of trade unions as follows:

> Parliament has conferred more freedom from restraint on trade unions than has ever been known to the law before. All legal restraints have been lifted so that they can now do as they will. Trade unions and their officers — and, indeed, groups of workmen, official or unofficial — are entitled to induce others to break their contracts — not only contracts of employment but other contracts as well — they are entitled to interfere and prevent the performance of contracts by others — all with impunity. Any such inducement or interference is not only not actionable at law. It is specifically declared to be 'not unlawful'. It is therefore proclaimed to be lawful, provided always this (and this is the one limit to the exemption which is conferred): it must be 'in contemplation or furtherance of a trade dispute'.

It is interesting to note the difference in standing at law between the modern corporation and the modern trade union.

When parliament allows groups of individuals to exercise such power it should come as no surprise that they use it for their own advantage and contrary to the public interest. On the basis of their legal privileges trade unions have created an economic power base through the use of two devices: the straightforward use of monopoly power and the threat of using the strike weapon. The two are different. The use of monopoly power obtained through the creation of closed shops, regulation of the terms of apprenticeship and so on is comparable to the use of monopoly power by corporations in a position to exercise it. It operates through market forces — a restriction in supply leads to an increase in the relevant price or wage. But the systematic use of the threat is comparatively recent. It works by disrupting the market and presenting the employer with a choice either to close operations or concede the union's demands. In view of their economic power, I believe that the trade unions in Britain today have five major consequences:

Firstly, individual trade unions raise the real wages of their members at the expense of non-unionised workers — in practice wages obtained by collective bargaining tend on average to be about 20 per cent higher than other wages. There are trade union leaders who see nothing wrong in this situation. Arthur Scargill put it that 'Whilst we exist in a capitalist society we have to extract from that society the highest possible reward for the labour power that we sell, whilst at the same time trying to change the society.'

In the second place, through the use of restrictive practices and their ability to veto industrial change, unions are a direct cause of low productivity and overmanning — which results in a loss of income for the nation as a whole.

Thirdly, by raising the level of wages above that at which they would otherwise be, the trade union movement bears a major responsibility for the high and increasing level of unemployment in the UK today.

Then through the use of secondary picketing, frequently associated with intimidation and physical violence (such as we have seen repeatedly over the past decade in connection with the miners' strikes, the Shrewsbury incidents, Grunwick, the lorry drivers' strike), unions become a threat to personal freedom.

Finally, because of the difficulty which individual workers find in withdrawing from closed shop agreements, individual liberty in this country is directly under attack from the unions.

As one reads the various strictures of the Old Testament prophets against those who exploit their economic power, I cannot help feeling that their major relevance within the UK today is to the trade union movement by the power exercised by elements within it.

Apart from their legal privileges which are frankly impossible to defend on the basis of a concept of Christian justice, there is also a strong argument against the whole idea of *collective* bargaining by contrast to individual wage setting. A collective bargain is based on the concept of power which is the reason that any trade union aspires to closed shop status. Unless a union is negotiating with a monopoly corporation or with companies which are collectively violating standards of decency and justice in their own employment practices, the outcome of such a bargain must of necessity be unjust. Take for example the level of wages and working practices of the print unions in Fleet Street which are so obviously the result of the use of naked power. Not only that but a collective bargain is a method of suppressing individual differences between workers. Rarely will two people doing the same job deserve the same wage. They have different productivities, make different contributions and so deserve to be remunerated differently. From a Christian point of view this is thoroughly desirable.

Reforming the Structures of the Market Economy

Doubtless there will be some who will argue that attempting to change structures is less important than trying to convince those who exercise power in our society to do so responsibly or that in any case radical changes in structures are politically impossible. As far as the latter is concerned, I am always surprised by how much of what is considered politically impossible today turns out to be quite acceptable tomorrow. Would any politician in the 1950s have admitted that double digit inflation, three million unemployed and interest rates of 15 per cent were a political possibility for the UK? Today that is reality. Or consider the growth of monetarism and the present government's rejection of short-term demand management and its adoption of a medium-term monetary fiscal plan as the cornerstone of its economic policies. Twenty-one years ago that would have been inconceivable. More than that I believe that what is right needs to be said. If this involves going back to first principles, then however removed they may be from our present experience, we have a responsibility to go back.

As far as the first point is concerned, there is I believe a real appeal for many people, not least on Christian grounds, in arguing that the overriding need at present in the UK is for the government, the TUC and the CBI to sit around a table and talk, so that both corporations and unions will change their behaviour and act in the public interest rather than their own self-interest. As a result it is argued, the rate of inflation could be reduced that much more rapidly and unemployment rise that much less. What could be more Christian than that?

I share a concern for the creation of a more stable and just society but I would argue against the adoption of such societies. We have now had in this country in the post war years six or seven 'contracts' drawn up between the triumvirate of the corporate state. On each occasion the initial stage has been a dramatic success and the final outcome a categorical failure — responsible in my judgment for the defeat both of Mr Heath's and Mr Callaghan's governments. The reason is not hard to find. By encouraging, cajoling, indicating and directing corporations and trade unions to act in the national interest rather than in their own self-interest, the government is counseling these institutions to behave in a way which is wholly inconsistent with their raison d'être, which in turn results from the property rights with which they are endowed. If our legal system allows companies the ability to make profits and trade unions to bargain collectively for wage increases, then we should not be surprised that companies will wish to exploit profit opportunities and trade unions secure higher wages whenever possible, however inconvenient at times that may be to the government. If we are concerned about excess profits, monopoly wages and unemployment we have to tackle the problem at root, namely by re-examining the structure of corporations, government and trade unions.

REFORMING THE CORPORATE STATE

Corporations

In response to the criticisms of the corporation which we considered earlier, various reforms have been put forward. Under the banner of industrial democracy various changes have been proposed in the structure of the organisation, decision-making and ownership of companies, involving things such as compulsory councils and co-determination at the shop-floor level, the representation of workers on the board, and most recently (in Sweden and Holland) the setting up of a union-controlled wage-earners' fund by capitalising a percentage of pretax profits, with the newly issued shares being placed in the fund and used to acquire interests in other companies and to supplement wages in the lowest-paid jobs. Some Christians have called for representation of workers on the board of directors, joint decision-making at all levels within the company, the break-up of oligopolies, a restriction on the number of director-ships any one person can hold (the suggested number is three) and restrictions on the directors of financial corporations holding directorships in non-financial corporations, and vice versa. Some companies have been set up and others reformed to offer an alternative to the limited liability structure, for example the John Lewis Partnership, the Scott Bader Co. Ltd, Landsman's (Co-ownership) Ltd, and the Meriden Motorcycle Cooperative. In France there are over five hundred worker cooperatives and in Mondragon in Spain, over fifty enterprises linked to a movement for worker ownership associated with Father Arizmendi, a Roman Catholic priest.

It is important that as Christians we conceive of the corpora-tion as a community which has as an objective more than just profit maximisation. The directorate of a company has a responsibility to those with whom they deal as people rather than just as instruments of profit. It is therefore important that management accept a responsibility to communicate the prospects, plans and performance of the organisation to the whole of its work force. A directorate and management will succeed only if they have the trust of those with whom they work – the need to develop a common involvement is important. But to go on from this to the recommendation of the Bullock Report that workers should have representation on a company's board is to change the nature of the institution, which in my judgment is quite unwarranted. A key element in the constitution of a company is the notion that all members of the board are responsible to the company as a whole. To make certain board members responsible to workers and presumbly others to suppliers, others to customers and others to the general public would change the board into a kind of parliament with members representing their various constituencies. The evidence from European countries of attempts to implement these kinds of arrangements tends to support the view that while they help ease labour-management tensions they slow down decision-making and reduce management flexibility. If full parity were ever granted, there is a fear that a deadlock could arise and that in addition certain directors might be forced to reveal business secrets to their constituents which could paralyse the operation.

The question of concentration is a more serious issue. The real issue here is not size per se but the degree of monopoly power and possible operating inefficiency which accompanies size. I believe there is enough direct evidence on the degree of monopoly power in this country in areas such as coal, postal services and banking to suggest that this is an important problem.

In terms of constructive policies to deal with the corporate sector, I would emphasise the following. There is a need for a more vigorous competition policy both in manufacturing industry and services but especially with respect to public sector monopolies, and for a change in fiscal policy to remove the artificial incentives which companies now have to retain earnings. Company and tax law should be amended to make it easier to set up diversified forms of ownership including profit-sharing schemes. All public companies should include non-executive directors on their boards. Audit committees are already strongly recommended for public companies. Taken together these could make a real contribution to improved corporate performance.

GOVERNMENT

In view of the Christian concern with human personality and individual responsibility and the importance of retaining areas

121

over which discretion is possible, it is imperative that the present growth of government in modern society be halted. But the critical question is whether the juggernaut of public expenditure can be brought under control. Various governments have come to office in the postwar years, some committed to reducing public spending, others to raising it. Regardless of intention, public expenditure as a proportion of national income has gone on rising. The present trend is nothing less than alarming. I confess that I am deeply pessimistic about halting and reversing the trend without legislative guidelines established by referenda which put limits on the growth of government expenditure or the growth of tax revenue. Without such constraints, democratically elected politicians face overwhelming pressures to spend, however good their intentions. In this respect, I have been influenced by the success of Proposition 13 enacted in California in 1978, which necessitated a sharp reduction in property taxes. In 1979 the state constitution was amended and a ceiling placed on spending by the state and in local jurisdictions within its borders. Comparable reforms have been introduced in a number of other states and a movement is growing to amend the Constitution of the United States to place comparable constraints on federal government activities.

Related to this is the question of the use of discretionary monetary and fiscal policy to stabilise the economy overall, and provide full employment and contain inflation. Ever since the Keynesian revolution of the thirties government has accepted these commitments. However successful these policies may have been in the fifties we have, I believe, convincing evidence that they have failed since the world-wide inflation which started with the mismanagement of the finances raised to pay for the Vietnam War. Unemployment and inflation have increased in one country after another and two of the most volatile and destabilising elements in our economies have turned out to be the size of the public sector deficit and the rate of growth of the money supply. As a result of the uncertainty generated in the private sector by expected movements in these variables the best that the public sector can do is to inform the private sector of its intentions and then act accordingly. This is the logic behind the Thatcher government's medium-term financial plan.

I would like to go further, however, and suggest that the best outcome would be if discretion over monetary policy were removed altogether from the hands of the Treasury and the Bank of England and legislated by Parliament in terms of a monetary rule. The rule could be made simple or complex and even a simple rule could be adjusted to deal with real shocks to the economy, such as from OPEC hikes in the price of oil. I have come to the view that the discretionary use of monetary and fiscal policy, even when constrained by monetary targets and financial plans, is likely to prove unsatisfactory because of the combination of political pressures and market pressures with which the authorities have to deal. Although this proposal has at present not the slightest chance of being implemented, nevertheless as the rate of inflation and growing unemployment prove to be intractable problems so people will be forced to seek solutions which work in practice even if that means constraining both government and its officials. It is interesting that in the last hundred years, periods of relatively stable prices were periods when the British government did not have discretionary control over money supply growth — namely the pre-First World War gold standard and the Bretton Woods System — whereas periods of inflation and deflation have occurred when the system is anchorless.

TRADE UNIONS

On grounds of Christian justice there is an overwhelming case in Britain today for a fundamental reform of the rights, privileges and responsibilities of trade unions. The object of reform should be to require of trade unions the same degree of responsibility within law that is at present required of corporations.

This is no small order. It requires the abolition of trade union immunities, the ending of legal protection for the 'closed shop', the introduction of legally enforceable collective agreements, the sequestration of trade union funds in cases in which secret

123

ballots have not been held in support of strike action, and the provision by trade unions of greater information regarding their financial affairs.

CONCLUSION

Let me now conclude. We have seen how the corporatist welfare state which has emerged in this country over the past hundred years is a reflection of a humanist philosophy in which the creation of wealth is of less concern and morally inferior than its distribution, in which the pursuit of equality has become the dominant economic philosophy and in which the state rather than the individual has come to be held responsible for solving our problems.

We have attempted to look at the three critical institutions of the corporate state and to examine their legitimacy in Christian terms. While the key features of each — the limited liability company, the use of collective bargaining and the state provision of welfare — all have something of a Christian basis in terms of providing outlets for savings, strengthening the family, and correcting injustice and providing for those in need, nevertheless it is easy to see how they can become taken over by humanistic philosophy — so that they become unlimited freedom to create wealth, the use of collective power and the denial of individual merit and the state as the alternative for the family and private charity.

From the point of view of social and economic policy I believe we face a choice: *either* we accept the present trends which will lead inevitably to a decline in individual freedom and responsibility and the restriction of opportunities for our children and grandchildren *or else* we face the seemingly impossible task of dismantling the corporate state. This is not an attempt to return to a nineteenth-century form of laissez-faire but to change the structures of our society in a direction more consonant with our Christian principles. And I believe it is something in which we should all be involved.

CHAPTER 5

THIRD WORLD POVERTY AND
FIRST WORLD RESPONSIBILITY

The starting point of these lectures has been the global conflict which exists today between capitalism and socialism. In the West capitalism has proved to be an efficient economic system, yet it seems to have lost its legitimacy. Historically this was provided by a Judaeo-Christian world-view which emphasised a sense of individual responsibility and justified the economic inequalities which result from the workings of the market place. Since the Enlightenment however, this world-view has been replaced by a humanist philosophy which makes freedom the absolute and which is impossible to justify in Christian terms. The alternative system is Marxism. In tracing the roots of Marxism we found that these too were grounded in an Enlightenment world-view — which rejects the uniqueness of man created in the image of God and the fact of a Fall, with all the limitations which it imposes on creating a Utopia. In practice we found the existence of two triads — the commitment to abolish the family, religion and private property — resulting almost invariably in a triad of outcomes — economic inefficiency, religious persecution and political terror. The choice between libertarian capitalism and Marxist socialism therefore is a choice between competing ideologies, both of which embody a humanistic world-view.

We then contrasted these with the Biblical revelation and found that this provided us with a distinctive alternative. In the previous chapter we examined contemporary economic society in the UK — the corporatist, welfare state — and found that there was at the centre of each of the elements of the corporate state an institution or practice fundamentally at variance with the

125

Christian ideal — be it limited liability, collective bargaining or state welfare. We argued that Christianity was relevant to the matter of reforming the market economy because it suggested an alternative to an increasingly large and more powerful corporate state. In this last lecture we turn to the problems of the Third World.

What is the Problem?

Since the middle of this century the performance of Third World countries in economic terms has been impressive. Income per person has grown by about 3 per cent a year. This record is not only far better than the historical record of these countries but also higher than that achieved by developed countries when they were at a comparable stage of development. From the mid-nineteenth to the mid-twentieth century income per person in the developed countries grew at less than 2 per cent a year. The increasing income of the developing countries has been accompanied by the process of industrialisation so that the share of agriculture in total production has fallen while that of industry and services has risen. The percentage of school-age children attending school has increased sharply, as has the literacy of the population. At the same time life expectancy has risen and infant mortality has fallen.

Despite such great progress, the existence of absolute poverty for many hundreds of millions of people involving malnutrition, illiteracy, disease and starvation is a fact of today's world. Robert McNamara, President of the World Bank, defined absolute poverty as 'a condition of life so characterised by malnutrition, illiteracy, disease, squalid surroundings, high infant mortality and low life expectancy as to be beneath any reasonable definition of human decency'.[1] Regardless of whether we are capitalist or Marxist, Christian or Hindu, or whether the colour of our skin is black, brown, white or yellow, absolute poverty remains a disturbing fact. In the early seventies the international Labour Office estimated that the very poor amounted to 700 million. More recently the World Bank puts the figure at 800 million. The number of undernourished and hungry is put at somewhere between 500–600 million and one billion.

Most of us in the West have no idea of what it must be like to live in such a situation of total deprivation with no or very little work, no adequate sanitation or clean water, economic insecurity, little if any formal education, inadequate health services, overcrowded housing, without either running water or electricity.

Yet for many of the rural population of India, Bangladesh, Pakistan, Indonesia and smaller countries such as Bhutan, Chad, Mali, Burundi and Cambodia this is the pattern of life. What is particularly disturbing is a recent World Bank estimate which suggests that even on the most favourable assumptions about economic growth, while the number of absolute poor are likely to decline by the end of the century, there could still remain as many as 600 million. The critical problem facing certain Third World countries, therefore, is the hundreds of millions of our fellow human beings who like us have been created in the image of God but who live in conditions of appalling deprivation.

Having accepted this, it is just as important for us also to recognise that the problem is one of poverty and not inequality. Inequality does not necessarily imply poverty, unless one defines poverty, as certain contemporary social scientists do, in terms of inequality. Because inequality per se is not the problem I find it unhelpful to talk about the widening gap between the developed and developing countries. There are three reasons. To start with, it makes no sense whatever to lump together over a hundred countries of the world which have different climates, natural resources, religions and political systems and which are at different stages of economic development, and then to label them the Third World, the LDCs (Less Developed Countries) or the Developing Countries. The only characteristic which they have in common is a per capita income less than some arbitrarily defined level. Next, comparison of per capita incomes between countries is beset by enormous problems. Estimates of population are unreliable, intra-family services tend to be underestimated and the exchange rates used for comparison between countries tend to understate the domestic incomes of developing countries.

Most important is the algebra of gaps. Assume two countries with incomes of 100 and 50 units in one year and 1000 and 900 in another. The absolute gap has doubled but the relative difference has been reduced by four fifths. Although poor countries grow faster than rich countries, the absolute gap will not even begin to fall until the ratio of their per capita incomes is equal to the inverse of the ratio of their growth rates. For example, although the Korean growth rate has been twice that of OECD countries for the past two decades, the absolute gap will continue to increase until the per capita income of Korea reaches one half that of the OECD countries. If we treat GNP statistics as accurate and project historical growth rates into the future, then for the fastest-growing LDCs only 8 will close the gap in 100 years and only 16 within 1000 years. In Malaysia it will take over 2000 years and in China nearly 3000 years. For the vast majority of LDCs the absolute gap will never be closed.

If one is interested in the absolute progress of the LDCs, the key welfare statistic is not the 'gap' but the absolute standard of living. Not only that but many LDCs would not wish to emulate Western countries. A respected official of the World Bank, Mahbub al Haq, has argued:

> The concept of catching up must be rejected. Catching up with what? Surely the Third World does not wish to imitate the life styles of the rich nations? It must meet its own basic human needs within the framework of its own cultural values, building development around people rather than people around development.

The Causes of Third World Poverty

It is important to begin by examining the cause of Third World poverty. The current most generally accepted explanation is that the poverty of the Third World results from its exploitation by the First World. The First World is rich because the Third World is poor. As a result of 'evil structures' such as neo-colonialism, tariff barriers and multi-national corporations, Western countries enjoy a high standard of living. This is the direct consequence of their extracting raw materials, food and cheap manufactured goods from Third World countries. At the same time they pay inadequate wages and earn excess profits on their investment in these countries. One of the great British authorities on poverty, Professor Peter Townsend, states:

The poverty of deprived nations is comprehensible only if we attribute it substantially to the existence of a system of international stratification, a hierarchy of societies with vastly different resources in which the wealth of some is linked historically and contemporaneously to the poverty of others. This system operated crudely in the era of colonial domination, and continues to operate today, though more subtly, through systems of trade education, political relations, military alliances and industrial corporations.[2]

In opening the UN World Population Conference in August 1974, President Nicolae Ceausescu of Rumania stated, 'The division of the world into developed and underdeveloped countries is a result of historical evolution and is a direct consequence of the imperialist, colonialist and neo-colonialist policies of exploitation of many peoples.'[3] The same theme has also emerged from Christians. Stanley Mooneham, President of World Vision International, talks of 'the stranglehold which the developed West has kept on the economic throats of the Third World.'[4] Julius Nyerere, the President of Tanzania, in a lecture in London in 1976 said:

In one world, as in one state, when I am rich because you are poor, and I am poor because you are rich, the transfer of wealth from the rich to the poor is a matter of right . . . if the rich nations go on getting richer and richer at the expense of the poor, the poor of the world must demand a change in the same way as the proletariat in the rich countries demanded a change in the past.[5]

In a section entitled 'Institutional Evil Today' of his book on world hunger Ronald Sider states:

We are all implicated in structural evil. International trade patterns are unjust. An affluent minority devours most of the earth's non-renewable natural resources. Food consumption patterns are grossly lopsided. And the returns on investment in poor countries are unjustly high. Every person in developed countries benefits from these structural injustices. Unless you have retreated to some isolated valley and grow or make everything you use, you participate in unjust structures which contribute directly to the hunger of a billion malnourished neighbours.[6]

In general terms I believe that the charge which these people make is almost entirely untrue. While I accept that in certain specific situations colonialism may have retarded development and that certain multi-nationals may have exploited a monopoly position, I believe that it is entirely false to suggest that the wealth of the West is at present being obtained at the expense of Third World countries or that the poverty of the Third World is the result of systematic exploitation by the West.

To start with, this whole thesis is an amalgam of classic British Fabianism linked to Lenin's theory of imperialism, in which the exploitation of the proletariat by the bourgeoisie has been replaced by the exploitation of the Third World by the First World. The fundamental assumption is that the process of wealth creation is a zero-sum game in which the increased income of some is only obtained by making others poorer, rather than a 'positive-sum game' in which the incomes of all participants are increased in the process of wealth creation. Within a Marxist framework anyone who uses privately owned capital to produce something is guilty of exploiting the workers by *definition*. As a result, the Third World is poor because the First World is rich, the wages of black Africa are low because of exploitation by multi-nationals, the starvation of Bangladesh is caused by the overeating of the West. The important point to notice is that in a Marxist framework exploitation is a characteristic of free markets *by definition*. By contrast the non-Marxist approach views the creation of wealth as a process of cooperation between the suppliers of funds, the owners of land, the services of managers and the skills of the labour force. By these various resources being put together profitably, wealth is created and all those involved in the wealth creation process enjoy a share of the increased wealth. Rates of wages and profit are determined by the basic forces of supply and demand and reflect the contribution which they make to the wealth creation process. Within this framework exploitation is certainly possible but it depends on the evidence and not on the assumptions. I would suggest that the only valid test of exploitation is whether foreign capital can systematically earn a higher rate of return in these countries than in the developed world or whether foreign companies can systematically exploit the labour market of Third World countries through their position as sole buyer of labour in given situations.

Let us consider the multi-nationals. The most important benefits to a developing country from foreign direct investment are firstly, the wages paid to local labour, secondly the tax revenues receives by the host government and thirdly, the expenditure by multi-nationals in purchasing local products. These three items are defined as the value added which is retained by the host government. Estimates of this are not easy to obtain but in a study for the OECD published in 1973, Grant Reuber, a distinguished Canadian economist, estimated that in 1957 the retained value added as a result of US direct investment in Latin America was 82.9 per cent of sales and that by 1966 this figure had increased to 90 per cent.[7] For the Far East excluding Japan the figure was 88 per cent. In Latin America 66 per cent of the retained value added was expenditure on local material and equipment, 18 per cent wages and salaries and17 per cent revenue. The International Labour Office of the United Nations in an estimate based on statistics in 1970 suggests that total tax revenue accruing to Third World governments was between $5.5 and $7.0 billion, which constituted approximately 3–4 per cent of their income.[8] There is also evidence to suggest that multi-nationals pay higher than average wage rates in Third World countries. In a sample of 23 multi-national investments in the Third World, Reuber found that 15 paid 1–10 per cent above the going wage rate and 8 more than 10 per cent. There are also benefits such as the training by foreign firms of skilled labour which are then employed by local firms, and the transfer of technology by entering into sub-contracting arrangements with local firms so providing them with technical assistance, which are difficult to quantify but which are nevertheless real.

In addition, returns on direct foreign investment in developing countries are not noticeably different from those in developed countries. For example, the Reddaway Report in the UK estimated that the average annual return on capital from UK manufacturing companies over the years 1965–8 was 9.8 per cent in the developed countries and 9.3 per cent in the developing countries.[9] For the US comparable figures suggest a remarkably similar outcome.[10]

TABLE 5

Rates of Return on US Foreign Private Investment
in Manufacturing (per cent)[11]

	1970	1975	1976	1977	1978
Developed countries	10.5	10.6	12.5	11.7	15.6
Developing countries	10.8	13.9	11.5	11.1	14.7

Note: Rate of return is defined as income (sum of dividend, interest payments, earnings of unincorporated affiliates) plus reinvested earnings of incorporated affiliates divided by the average of the beginning and the end of the year stock of foreign private investment.

Two ways in which multi-nationals are specifically alleged to exploit LDCs are pricing imported technologies above the true cost and depriving the host government of tax revenue by transfer pricing — that is by moving profits geographically by accounting for them as costs of transferring resources to a subsidiary firm. As far as the first is concerned direct evidence is hard to come by. The rationale for charging for imported technology is partly as a return to the investment which the parent company has made in research and development and partly because of the costs in transferring the technology. In a study of 26 transfer projects which related to chemicals, petroleum refining and machinery industries, costs of transferring technology averaged 19 per cent of the total cost of the project and varied between 2 per cent and 59 per cent. This is not to say that in certain cases technology may not be overpriced and this is a matter which requires greater disclosure of information by corporations. Transfer pricing has certainly been used by some firms to minimise the global costs of their operation. The major reason for this practice is differences in tax rates, tariffs and dividend policies between countries, which raises the whole issue of the harmonisation of fiscal structures between countries. We shall deal with these issues later. But on the basis of such evidence as exists it would, I think, be difficult to make out a case alleging that the multi-nationals have systematically exploited Third World countries.

Lastly, there is the charge that because the multi-nationals employ capital-intensive methods of production they tend to transfer inappropriate technology to the Third World and so do not create a great deal of employment in these countries. A UN commission has estimated that in 1976 direct employment by foreign affiliates of multi-nationals was between 3–4 million, equivalent to 1 per cent of the labour force.[12] However, investment by multi-nationals in the Third World is highly concentrated in certain countries such as Brazil, Mexico, South Korea, Singapore and Hong Kong and in these countries employment is significant. In 1970 employment by multinationals in Brazil accounted for 8.5 per cent of total manufacturing employment and in Mexico 9.9 per cent. In another study Watanobe suggests that the major factor responsible for reducing the South Korean unemployment rate from 8.1 per cent in 1963 to 4.7 per cent in 1970 was exported growth, a great deal of which was the result of investment by foreign firms.[14]

As far as inappropriate technology is concerned there are a number of studies which show that foreign firms are less capital-intensive than domestic firms. Studies undertaken in Kenya and Brazil (one by the International Labour Office) show that foreign firms were less capital-intensive than domestic firms and that the major reason was superior management. A major reason for inappropriate technology seems to be the adoption by countries of industrial policies, such as the development of import-substitute producing industries, which allows firms to earn adequate profits without the stimulus provided by competition.

Next consider the indictment of colonialism as part of the general charge that Third World poverty is the result of First World prosperity. I have no brief to defend the colonial record of Western and Eastern nations but as Professor P.T. Bauer has courageously argued for many years it is fanciful to think that colonialism is an adequate explanation of Third World poverty. In general terms quite the opposite is true: those countries which have had most contact with the West (eg, cash-crop areas and entrepôt ports of South-East Asia, West Africa and Latin America and mining areas in Africa and the Middle East) are the most advanced economically, while those with little contact are the least advanced (Afghanistan, Tibet, Nepal and Liberia, none of which were colonised); contact with the West led in such areas as West Africa and South-East Asia to the introduction of public health, hospitals, better transport, improved technology and education. In any case if this thesis were generally true it would be difficult to explain the wealth of

Canada, Switzerland and Sweden which have not had colonies or the remarkable growth of Hong Kong which remains a British colony.

Yet another variant of this charge is that the West has rigged the structure and terms of international trade to its own advantage and to the disadvantage of the LDCs. It is quite wrong to suggest that the international trading system is a sort of jungle in which the strong systematically exploit the weak. The basic structure of international trade is fundamentally a good one. It depends on institutions such as the General Agreement on Tariffs and Trade which was set up after the Second World War and which has been responsible for the major reduction in world tariff barriers (in a series of bargaining rounds, the most recent being the Tokyo round), and the OECD Codes of Liberalisation in the fields of invisible trade and capital movements which have been responsible for greater freedom for capital flows. The object has been to establish an international economic order in which countries are free to trade with each other and in which barriers to trade between countries are as low as possible. The major obstacle to achieving this is the behaviour of national governments, which resort either to the use of tariffs, quotas and agreements to restrict trade in order to protect their domestic industries or to cartel agreements, such as OPEC which distort prices to their own advantage simply because of their greater bargaining power. It is these rather than the structure of the GATT based on the principles of free trade which are basic injustices of the world economy today.

Although the world trading system is fundamentally sound the less developed countries do have a number of legitimate grounds for complaint at present. The major ones are: high US and European protection in textile products: subsidies to declining industries such as steel, shipbuilding, footwear and clothing in European countries; the Common Agricultural Policy of the European Economic Community which protects, in particular, French and German farmers at great cost, raises the price of food to European consumers and results in surpluses in the form of butter mountains and surplus sugar,

135

and a high rate of effective protection on processed products, examples being unprocessed rice which enters the EEC free of duty while processed rice faces a 13 per cent tariff; on variable import levies on untreated wood which enters Australia free, while sawn timber faces a tariff of 14 per cent.

The exploitation thesis may be summed up as follows. In general terms it is impossible to accept the thesis that the poverty of the Third World is the result of the prosperity of the First World. The Third World has certain legitimate grievances against the First World but at best these are marginal in explaining Third World poverty. What is not generally recognised is that the currently fashionable quasi-Marxist framework within which Third World problems are being analysed is counter productive to the real plight of the distressed in these countries. It is counter productive because it has resulted in the wholesale politicisation of the issues involved. The major issue of poverty has been changed very subtly to a discussion of inequality, the focus is on groups, classes and nations but rarely the plight of individuals: the material is emphasised to the conclusion of the immaterial, the causes of poverty are external factors but rarely home grown, and finally the responsibility is shifted from individuals to governments. Put bluntly, it totally distorts and undermines a Christian perspective on global poverty.

What then is the explanation for poverty? The traditional economic approach to answering this question — the neoclassical economic growth model — emphasises the role of natural resources, capital investment, technology, innovation and the size and skill of the labour force. Geography and natural resources are important as is clear from the phenomenal increase in the per capita wealth of the OPEC countries since 1973. The US, Canada and Australia have considerable endowment of natural resources which is doubtless part of the explanation for their wealth. But countries such as Zaire also have substantial natural resources, but they remain largely unexploited. Not only that but there are many wealthy countries in Western Europe and elsewhere which have very limited mineral deposits and rather restricted fertile land like Germany and

Switzerland and in the East, Hong Kong. The fortunes of geography are important but by no means decisive.

Another explanation has to do with the lack of capital. Frequently the argument is put forward that the lack of foreign investment in Third World countries is discrimination by the developed neo-colonialist powers against developing countries. As far as capital investment is concerned, however, the interesting question is why investment proceeds at very different rates in different Third World countries. Why is it that over the past two decades countries such as Brazil and South Korea have had no difficulty in obtaining capital whereas countries such as many sub-Saharan African countries have found it virtually impossible to persuade foreigners to invest?

Before discrimination is brought in as an explanation, it is valuable to examine the political instability, the rate of inflation, the kinds of foreign exchange controls, the level and structure of taxes and the threat of nationalisation in these countries which suffer from a lack of capital.

The critical factor is not overall discrimination or a general 'shortage' of funds available to Third World countries. It is far more basic than that. It is a lack of suitable investment opportunities, either because certain necessary skills are lacking or because the government has created a hostile environment for foreign capital. A high-ranking World Bank official with a great deal of experience in Third World countries summed it up as follows:

Over the post war period immense sums have been made available to the developing areas. Some of these funds have been well applied and have produced sound results, others have not . . . If [money] is applied to uneconomic purposes, or if good projects are poorly planned and executed, the results will be minus not plus. The effective spending of large funds requires experience, competence, honesty and organisation. Lacking any of these factors, large injections of capital into developing countries can cause more harm than good. The fact of how much additional capital is required for devel-

137

opment is how much a country can effectively apply within a given period, not how much others are willing to supply.[15]

This view clearly suggests that the insights which are yielded by traditional economic analysis, although useful, are limited.

When we look at the history of an economy over a long period of time, or at economies with vastly differing income levels and institutions, we are forced to consider factors which are not given great emphasis in traditional economic analysis. I am sure that E.F. Schumacher is correct when he states in his book *Small is Beautiful* that 'The primary causes of extreme poverty are immaterial, they lie in certain deficiences in education, organisation and discipline.'[16]

In this same vein Robert L. Garner who was Vice-president of the World Bank and President of the International Finance Corporation has put it as follows:

I am forced to the conclusion that economic development or lack of it is primarily due to differences in people — in their attitudes, customs, traditions and the consequent difference in their political, social and religious institutions.[17]

I would like to start by arguing like Schumacher and Garner that the poverty of Third World countries is principally non-economic in origin.

Although this is a complex subject it is possible to class non-economic factors into a number of separate categories: political factors, the choice of economic system and culture. Political factors include corruption, racial discrimination, extravagance and incompetence on the part of governments. In the world of the UN, UNCTAD and among the aid lobbies of the Western world, these are taboo subjects. But for Third World countries they are a reality. Earlier this century Argentina was among the top ten richest countries in the world but as a result of Peronism it has been thrust into underdevelopment. Nkrumah in Ghana, Nyerere in Tanzania, Touré in Guinea, Amin in Uganda have all impoverished their countries by appalling political mismanagement. By contrast Kenya and Ivory Coast which were well governed have been far from prosperous. The International Monetary Fund in a recent report was highly critical of the way in which aid has been administered in Bangladesh. Some Third World governments have pursued high discriminatory racial policies — for example, regarding Asians in East Africa and Chinese in Malaysia. The Colonels who ruled Peru from 1968 to 1979 lowered gross production by more than 50 per cent in this period. These are not isolated examples. The tragedy is that they could be multiplied many times over for other Third World countries.

Just consider the case of Trinidad, a rich country with large oil and natural gas reserves and fertile arable land. Despite this the country has achieved just a fraction of its potential. Water reaches villages intermittently, unemployment is high, roads are in disrepair, health services have reached crisis proportions and good arable land is lying fallow. For the past twenty-five years Trinidad has been ruled very autocratically by Eric Williams who was determined to hold on to power while he lived: to achieve that he gerrymandered the voting system and took control of the civil service.

A prominent and respected Trinidad laywer, Mr Hudson-Phillips, said of the running of the country that 'The order of the day became . . . a country run by men who were taking the cream off the top, so much so that every deal that they made was done simply for the money they could pocket. And the foreign companies knew this, consequently they never felt a need to make their projects work. I'm not saying that every foreign company has failed but certainly most of them have.' A.N. Robinson, who was a founding member of Williams's party, has said:

'Third World countries have no protection against the politics of the cult of personality. A man like Eric Williams was able to become an absolute ruler in his time because his ascendancy to power was like a second emancipation. We had no institutions that could act as a buffer against his completely autocratic rule. He reached down into every facet of life, even

139

so far as to giving approval for middle-echelon civil servants to go on vacations that they were entitled to by law.

Trinidad is just one example. But the main point which needs to be emphasised with all political factors, is that they are a result of the deliberate choice of the countries concerned and that therefore these countries must also take direct responsibility for the consequences which follow.

A second factor which can either help or hinder economic development is a country's choice of economic system. By and large it can be said that economic systems which involve substantial state ownership, detailed government involvement in markets and some form or other of centralised planning tend to produce inefficient economies. By comparison economic systems which tap the resources of private enterprise, welcome foreign capital, allow incentives to work and minimise government involvement in markets tend to produce far more efficient economies. One of the saddest features of sub-Sahara Africa in the 1970s is the number of countries with *negative* per capita growth rates — Zaire, Zambia, Angola, Mozambique. But all of these countries have deliberately rejected the route of the market economy, choosing instead much government involvement and very much greater regulation.

The last factor is the culture of the peoples concerned. One does not have to accept the Tawney–Weber thesis in detail to accept the proposition that Biblical Christianity presents a distinctive and positive view of the material world and of the Christian's responsibilities in it; something which is in great contrast to that provided by other religions. Most people think of Weber's ideas only in terms of *The Protestant Ethic and the Spirit of Capitalism*. However, in his two other major works in this area, namely *The Religion of China* and *The Religion of India,* he contrasts a Biblically based Protestantism with Confucianism and Taoism in China and Hinduism in India.[18] And the contrast is quite striking. In Calvinism the world exists for the glory of god; the Christian is to serve God in all spheres of his life; work is seen as a calling but the pursuit of wealth a temptation, the Christian is 'in' the world but not 'of' the world; as a result activity, self-discipline, diligence and frugality are the virtues which are praised. This religious world-view fits in easily with an economic system which is based on the concept of rationality.

Rationality is something common to Confucianism but the rationality of Confucianism is of a fundamentally different kind: it is a rational materialism not a rational asceticism. For Confucianism the world is the best of all possible worlds and human nature disposed to be good. But the world is also imbued with magic. Salvation consists in adjusting to the eternal orders of the world in order to realise cosmic harmony. Although Confucianism is concerned with the creation of wealth and the material world rather than a life of asceticism, contemplation and mortification, nevertheless Confucian rationalism means a rational adaptation *to* the world, and it is a world which includes an element of magic. As the emperor is responsible for the good conduct of the spirits and ancestor worship is important to the formal practice of religion, it also involves an adjustment not just to the physical world but to traditional society as well. By contrast rationalism for the Puritan meant mastery over the world not submission to it. The anchor of Confucian ethics is magic; that of Protestant Christianity a revealed God. As a result Confucianism paid great respect to tradition, with the ideal of the individual reaching out for self-perfection and accepting the conventions of traditional society. By contrast the Christian was intent on pleasing God and as this involved his mind, his task was 'to work the works of him that sent him while it is day' not on the basis of ritual, but through the sanctified use of reason. Unlike Christian philosophy, Confucian philosophy could never provide a framework within which the process of industrialisation could successful develop.

Hinduism is very different from Confucianism. It is not concerned with wealth. For the Hindu the world is deterministic. The pursuit of knowledge is the path to the highest holiness. However, such knowledge is not communicable and can only be experienced mystically. As a result a life of contemplation and asceticism in which the soul can escape to a higher level is the basic ritual. The whole orientation of Hinduism, therefore, is to the irrational and the mystical — a concern for the inner self — with a passive view of the physical world but totally unconcerned with any concept of rational conduct in it. Out of this grew a very rigid social system in which apparent injustice to those who are poor and lacking in privilege was mitigated by the possibility of reincarnation.

In a very interesting book, A. Van Leeuwen analysed in greater detail the difference between cultures.[19] His starting point is the observation that Judaism is in many ways very different from other 'primitive' religions of Old Testament times. These emphasised a belief in a universal order of nature which nevertheless embraced diversity within a cosmic totality; the development into polytheism; the presence of magic; participation in a cyclical rhythm of nature rather than the purposeful movement of history to a definite event; and the longing for a complete fusion between man and nature so leading to a retreat into some form of mysticism. By contrast there is something very 'modern' about Judaism. More generally there is the contrast between a theocratic and an ontocratic culture: the former is a personal creator, whose existence is separate from his creation and who reveals himself in the Torah; the latter portrays the world as a primordial one in which nature partakes of divinity. As a result there is no distinction between God and nature, and so the natural world is to be worshipped. It would be sacrilege to apply technology to such a world. Because history has no purpose and the rhythm of nature and time is cyclical there is a changelessness about the world and a fate which takes away freedom from man. Ontocratic cultures therefore produce a world-view which is passive, resigned, submissive and customary while theocratic cultures produce one which is resourceful, evaluative, creative and innovative.

I use the writings of Tawney, Weber and Van Leeuwen to illustrate one basic point. If we really wish to understand the origins of poverty in Third World countries, I believe we are driven back to an examination of the culture of different countries and to asking basic questions. Why is it that in some societies individual human beings have the views of the physical world, of the importance of work, and the sense of self-discipline which they do? Why is it that in other societies they do not? Why is it that in some societies the institutions of the society are conducive to economic development while in others they are not? Personally, I find it impossible to answer these questions satisfactorily in purely economic terms. It is at this point that economic analysis needs a religious dimension.

Because of this I find it impossible to accept Willy Brandt's introductory statement to his report that 'we take it for granted that all cultures deserve equal respect, protection and promotion'. At first sight it seems that this view is positively Christian. But after some thought I believe the opposite to be the case. While all cultures deserve respect they do not all deserve equal protection and promotion. In the Old Testament the people of Israel were solemnly warned time and time against syncretism. Similarly the New Testament stands over and against all cultures. I am not suggesting that present Western culture, impregnated as it is with secular humanism, is to be preferred to other cultures. The first two chapters of this book were an attempt to demonstrate the failure of secular humanism even in its own terms. But to the extent that any culture contains Judaeo-Christian values, then surely those facets of that culture deserve especial protection and promotion.

Is the West Guilty? Is the West Responsible?

In the light of these arguments I believe we need to return once again to the question of the guilt and responsibility of the First World for and to the Third World. Subject to certain caveats which I have mentioned, I find it very difficult to accept that the West is in any direct way the cause of the poverty in the Third World. The international trading and monetary systems which we have at present are fundamentally sound, though the use of protection by both the developed and incidentally the developing countries, is something which is both inefficient and unjust. Direct foreign investment in the Third World largely through multi-national corporations is a vital source of wealth, employment and tax revenue for these countries. It is an efficient method of channelling human as well as physical capital to these countries and therefore an indispensable instrument for raising global income and wealth. Similarly the international banking system and the international capital markets have effectively channelled the OPEC countries' balance of payments surpluses to the LDCs in order to finance their deficits. As a consequence external debt as a percentage of GNP has risen sharply over the seventies in both low-income and middle-income countries. If debts had not increased in this way the alternative would have been greater recession and unemployment in these countries.

Having said this, there is no cause for smugness. Even if the West is not responsible for creating the poverty of the Third World, the Christian community in the West should most certainly feel a responsibility for alleviating the poverty of the Third World, for speaking out against injustice and for helping to establish more equitable structures and policies.

The New International Economic Order and the Brandt Report

During the last decade two major proposals have been put forward to help solve the problems of the Third World. In April 1974 the UN passed a resolution

> to work urgently for the establishment of a new international economic order based on equity, sovereign equality, common interest and cooperation among all stages, irrespective of their economic and political systems, which shall correct inequalities and redress existing injustices, make it possible to eliminate the widening gap between the developed and developing countries and ensure steadily accelerating economic and social development and peace and justice for present and future generations.

144

The old order was conceived of as capitalism and imperialism, followed in the post World War Two years by the Bretton Woods system within the world economy, and more recently by the Pax Americana by which the US has sought to provide a lead for the whole world. In their resolution of 1974 the UN included a number of specific economic proposals: the establishment of a common fund to stabilise commodity prices; the reduction of tariff barriers; the right of countries to nationalise foreign firms; an increase in aid (the target set was 0.7 per cent for developed countries); rescheduling and cancelling of debt; the transfer of technology independently of the multi-national corporations; and the reform of the international monetary system with greater participation for Third World countries linked to schemes for foreign aid. It did more than this however, it also implicitly proposed an enlarged role for the UN and its various agencies with very much greater executive power than at present.

The proposals for a New International Economic Order (NIECO) however ran into enormous protest from the First World. There were three major objections. Firstly, there was resentment at the hostility and even bitterness with which the proposals treated both capitalism and colonialism. Next, it appeared that the proposals were an attempt to extend the politicisation of economic life in order to create a global corporatist welfare state. Daniel Moynihan, then US Ambassador to the UN, put it succinctly: 'What is going on is the systematic effort to create an international society in which government is the one and only legitimate institution.'[19] Thirdly, the major purpose of the proposals was the distribution of wealth from the First World to the Third World rather than the creation of greater wealth for the world as a whole. This was true of the aid proposals, the commodities stabilisation scheme and the plans to reform the international monetary system. The role of property rights and markets was seen purely in terms of the distribution of income rather than in terms of their efficiency in creating wealth.

The Brandt Commission Report must be seen as a serious

attempt to tackle the same problem but without the vindictiveness of earlier proposals and with greater realism.[20] It is impossible to do justice to the Report in a short space but three aspects deserve attention: its fundamental value assumptions, its diagnosis of global problems and its major prescriptions. Although they are not set out explicitly in any particular section of the report it is nevertheless possible to detect a number of critical assumptions on which the report is built. One is the way in which poverty and development are reduced to a purely economic level, so that cultural differences become irrelevant: 'We take it for granted that all cultures deserve equal respect, protection and promotion.' Another is the mistrust of the working of free markets and the faith in regulation imposed by government, especially in the fields of energy, commodities and financial markets. Yet another is the sense of social engineering which emerges: the world is a Global Village whose problems have known technical solutions which can be readily applied by the village council. With great confidence the Report can ask 'What limits our response to this challenge on which the destiny of mankind depends?' and then answer 'Not primarily the technical solutions, *which are largely already familiar,* but the non-existence of a clear and generalised awareness of the realities and dangers and the absence of political will to face up to them and take corrective action.'

From these assumptions, the Report diagnoses two key problems in the world today: the way in which the income gap between the rich and poor exacerbates the crucial problems of the threat of world war, the deterioration of the environment and the breakdown of the world economy; and the fact that the major cause of world poverty is the present international economic order. On the basis of this diagnosis and of a recognition of the mutuality of interest between North and South, the Report then goes on to make a large number of specific policy recommendations, the major ones of which are that there should be a massive transfer of resources from the First to the Third World, a new set of rules within which multi-national corporations are allowed to operate, a reform of the inter-

146

national monetary system linked to increased foreign aid, and a reduction of trade barriers by the First World. Taken together, these amount to the construction of a global welfare state based on an automatic system of taxation.

It is not easy for a Christian to be seen to be critical of the Brandt Report. As Dudley Seers, a well known development economist at Sussex University, remarked, 'Pity the poor critic of the Brandt Report. To find fault with it looks almost as ungenerous as attacking the work of the International Red Cross.' The intention which lay behind it — the quest for peace, justice and prosperity as part of a programme for global survival — is admirable. Yet it is difficult not to have serious reservations about its analysis with the result that its policy recommendations seem inadequate and in part irrelevant to the achievement of its declared objectives.

To start with, the case against the present international economic order is assumed rather than proved. Nowhere does the Report show *how* the present international order reduces Third World countries to poverty or *why* some Third World countries have grown at a remarkable rate over the past decade while others have languished if the international economic order acts as a general constraint or development. Similarly, the effects of the North-South Gap as an obstacle to disarmament, a threat to the environment and a cause of the chronic pessimism of the world economy, are never demonstrated but simply taken for granted. The concept of mutuality which is rightly emphasised in this connection is, however, extremely vague. It is not true that the revival of growth in the North (which could read West) is dependent on the more rapid development of the South. It depends, as it has in the past, on Western governments pursuing appropriate policies and on the West recapturing a culture which is conducive to development. Similarly, massive transfers of resources from North to South are unlikely to solve the twin problems of high inflation and rising unemployment in Western countries by somehow stimulating export growth. This is Keynesianism but on a global scale. It is just the kind of policy which has failed signally in

Western countries to cure these very problems and there seems very little chance that they will work at a global level when they have failed at a national level.

The Report also fails to give sufficient emphasis to the need for reforms *within* Third World countries. At this point the Report displays the double standards which are typical of much development debate — the governments of the rich countries are attacked vehemently, those of the poor countries very little. I cannot emphasise enough that massive transfers to the Third World coupled with a Third World oriented reform of the international economy is neither a necessary nor a sufficient condition for more rapid development in the South: by comparison internal reforms in these countries are not only necessary, but also sufficient to achieve this purpose.

I believe that there are some very serious economic criticisms to be made of these proposals. But from a Christian point of view there is a more searching criticism yet. Throughout these lectures I have been at pains to point out one crucial fact; namely that the attempt to establish an economic system based on a humanist philosophy — whether of a libertarian or a Marxist variety — is doomed to failure even when considered in human terms. The Kingdom of God is not synonymous with low tax rates, higher productivity, free markets and a smaller public sector. But neither is it equivalent to collective ownership, egalitarianism, the welfare state and worker democracy. As one reads the UN proposals for a NIBO and the Brandt Commission Report, recommendations for peace, justice and more jobs, one cannot escape the feeling that both sets of proposals are shot through with a thoroughly humanist philosophy. They have a decidedly utopian ring about them. They pay scant attention to the spiritual roots of our economic problems. They totally ignore the relationship between economic structures and and economic philosophy. As a consequence their proposals for new structures are put forward in the context of a religious pluralism which is thoroughly humanist. 'We take it for granted that all cultures deserve equal respect, protection and promotion.' But they do not. Cultures

148

express values which shape institutions and motivate people —
some of which as we have seen promote wealth and justice and
liberty and others of which do not. Of course I recognise that
the Brandt Commission Report makes some very useful
recommendations. I welcome these but as a Christian I believe
that what is left out is critical.

Christian Imperatives for Third World Poverty

The Creation of Wealth

Third World governments have a crucial role to play in the
creation of wealth. At any particular time the culture, skills
infrastructure and natural resources of a country have to be
taken as given however much we may wish to improve them.
But Third World governments, through the economic policies
which they pursue, can either encourage or retard growth. By
limiting the growth of public expenditure, setting low average
and marginal tax rates, controlling the growth of the money
supply and therefore the rate of inflation, allowing markets to
work and offering reasonable terms to foreign investment,
Third World governments can encourage the creation of wealth.
Consider the successful economic performance of Brazil,
Mexico or Hong Kong, Singapore, Korea or Taiwan, all of
which have tapped the powerful resources of free enterprise.
Then consider the economic problems of India, Indonesia,
Angola, Mozambique and Tanzania. In each of these countries
the government has explicitly rejected private enterprise and the
market economy and chosen instead to go the route of public
enterprise and the planned economy. In each case the outcome
in economic terms can only be labelled a failure.

Next, as far as the creation of wealth is concerned, there is the
issue of the multi-national corporations. Earlier we saw that the
presence of the multi-nationals in Third World countries is an
important source of income, employment and tax revenue. But
we also saw that the existence of 'intra-firm' trade in which
transfer prices are established which are different from the

prices of competitive markets, can clearly be to the disadvantage of Third World countries. And in addition, multi-nationals have been criticised for unethical activities: such as the part they played in bringing down the Allende regime in Chile; the bribes given by various companies to Third World governments; and the way in which they support totalitarian regimes.

Over the past fifteen years or so, and as a response to the growth of multi-nationals, most Third World countries have introduced legislation to restrict their activities. It is quite wrong therefore to think of the multi-nationals as accountable to no one but their shareholders. They are accountable to regulatory bodies within Third World situations. Nevertheless the present situation is unsatisfactory because Third World governments distrust the intention of the companies, and the multi-nationals themselves fear the possibility of nationalisation without adequate compensation. It is clearly impossible in the immediate future to establish an international regulatory framework which has legal status and in any case the desirability of establishing some elaborate regulatory agency needs to be carefully examined. Regulation can be a very blunt instrument of control and if the terms are too onerous the multi-nationals will simply reduce their investment in Third World countries.

A better approach is the development of codes or guidelines. In 1976 the OECD adopted *Guidelines for Multinational Enterprices* which dealt with corporations in the OECD area. Since 1972 (UNCTAD III, in Santiago, Chile) the UN has been developing a code and a new UN Commission on the Transnational Corporation has been set up. At the same time a Code on Technology Transfer is also nearing completion. Such a code would, I believe, deal inter alia with a number of issues. It would recognise the legitimacy of both governments and multi-nationals to share the benefits of exploiting natural resources and the creation of wealth through the production of manufactured goods and services; recognising in particular the responsibility of government to honour contracts with multi-nationals on the transfer of profits, royalties, dividends and repatriation of capital. It would restrict the use of monopoly power and restrictive practices (in much the same way as First World governments deal with these problems). It would insist on a minimum of disclosure of information regarding 'intro-firm' practices. It would allow for some procedure to deal with cases under dispute. It would stipulate the general terms for compensation in the event of nationalisation.

The acceptance by governments of both First and Third World countries of such a code would, therefore, provide a framework within which the multi-nationals could legitimately function. It would extend into the field of direct investment something which has been accepted in the field of trade through the GATT and in the fields of invisible and capital movements through the OECD Codes of Liberalisation and the articles of the International Monetary Fund for many years.

For the Christian, however, unlike the professional economist, the concern with the creation of wealth does not end with the concern over the policies of Third World governments and the regulatory environment of multi-nationals. There must be the sense of personal responsibility.

There is in the First World a Christian community which contains many businessmen with a sense of responsibility, conscious of their privileged position and concerned to do something to help. There are in the Third World many possible projects which could be well served by such expertise. In a small way the International Institute for Development, Inc., in Washington DC, has been set up to act as a brokerage organisation between the perception by missionaries of possible ventures and Christians in the US who are interested in involvement. The aim is not for foreigners to establish a permanent equity interest in these ventures but to help set them up and then withdraw. I believe that the Christian business community in the First World needs a vision of what might be accomplished in this way.

Justice and Trading Structures

Next there is the question of justice and the world's trading structures. The quest for a more just international trading structure is a legitimate Christian concern. By being a member of the EEC Britain is, I believe, part of a system of protection which systematically penalises Third World countries. Consider the case of sugar. The production and export of sugar, mainly cane, has been a primary source of income for a number of Third World countries, like Mauritius, Fiji, the Dominican Republic, Philippines, Jamaica, Guatemala and Guyana for many years. However, by 1978 the world's major exporter of sugar after Cuba was the EEC. Through its highly protectionist policy the EEC has aimed at self-sufficiency in sugar by providing prices for EEC farmers which have been on average above the world price. The result has been a substantial sugar surplus which has then been dumped on the world market. The EEC keeps out cheaply produced foreign sugar by a high tariff but has agreed import quotas for those countries which are signatories to the Lome Agreement. The EEC has consistently refused to join the International Sugar Agreement because members would have to agree to export quotas at a time of low prices. The whole purpose of the EEC policy is primarily to protect the farming communities especially of France and Germany. The land used for sugarbeet production however could be turned to other profitable uses — though in this event they would not receive the subsidies currently received from sugar. This is a case where there is neither moral nor economic justification for what is happening. It is economically inefficient and it creates a perverse redistribution of income. But the case for sugar is not a typical example. As Christians we should be concerned to change this situation and I would like to say how much I applaud the work of such organisations as the Open Seas Forum and the World Development Movement in their campaign to reduce protectionism.

Development Aid and Relief

Next we come to the subject of development aid and relief. I believe there are only two reasonable defences of aid and relief, first as an act of charity from rich to poor countries and second because it is in the self-interest of the donor. Arguments about aid being necessary because of the inadequacy of the international capital market and its role in the development process seem to me to be dubious. Individually and collectively we have a responsibility to give because we see people in need. As Christians the great commandment which we are to obey is 'to love our neighbour as ourselves'. In a world which through remarkable technical progress has been reduced to a global village, we are forced to make neighbourhood global. And when one considers the numbers of those who are living in conditions of extreme poverty, the millions of people who are fleeing as refugees from the most inhumane regimes or are the victims of national disasters, like the Good Samaritan we have only to open our eyes and look around us to realise who are our neighbours in need.

The next question is, should aid be official or channelled through private agencies? I have to confess that I find real problems with government to government aid, which someone once described as a tax levied on the poor in rich countries to subsidise the rich in poor countries. Any government receiving aid is under great pressure to use it to further its own political self-interests rather than channel it to those most in need. By increasing the resources under government control, aid only encourages the politicisation of economic life in Third World countries. In addition it fosters a philosophy of dependency in which real income is increased by demanding, rather than producing more. It is for these reasons, that even among those in favour of aid, the 'basic needs' approach has arisen, which claims that aid is less likely to be used for political reasons if it is channelled towards satisfying the 'basic needs' of countries' small-scale agriculture projects, the choice of labour-intensive technology, local public health care, improvements to village schools and slum housing. I believe that aid has much greater appeal when it is seen to be relieving genuine poverty rather than supporting the construction of new capitals, increased bureaucracies and such things as independent national airlines and other so-called necessary conditions for more rapid development. If official aid is to be given, it should certainly be conditional. The fundamental question is whether it should be given at all, and the problem left to be solved by private charities.

World Evangelism

So far we have considered the creation of wealth, justice and charity. Lastly we turn to evangelism. I believe the place of evangelism as part of First World Responsibility to the problem of Third World poverty has been understated. Living as we do in an age in which a vague humanistic philosophy has become the dominant religion of the Western world, we as Christians seem increasingly reluctant to emphasise those features of our faith which distinguish us from non-Christians. But Our Lord's Great Commission still stands: 'Go into all the world and preach the gospel to the whole creation.' The Lausanne Covenant defines evangelism as:

The proclamation of the historical, biblical Christ as Saviour and Lord, with a view to persuading people to come to him personally and so be reconciled to God. In issuing the gospel invitation we have no liberty to conceal the cost of discipleship. Jesus still calls all who would follow him to deny themselves, take up their cross and identify themselves with his new community. The results of evangelism include obedience to Christ, incorporation into his church and responsible service in the world.

Christianity starts with faith in Christ and it finishes with service in the world. Although not its object, it is nevertheless, its inevitable consequence. Because of this I believe that evangelism has an indispensable part to play in the establishment of a more just economic order. Obedience to Christ demands change, the world becomes his world, the poor, the weak and the suffering are men, women and children created in his image; injustice is an affront to his creation; despair, indifference and aimlessness are replaced by hope, responsibility and purpose; and above all selfishness is transformed to love.

I believe that more than anything else this is what people the world over are looking for. It will not be found in either capitalism or Marxism but only through humility and obedience to Christ. But having found it in the most personal and intimate of all encounters, the most remarkable thing is that it is relevant to the social, political and economic problems even of the late twentieth century.

NOTES
Chapter 1
The Crisis of Capitalism

1. Fred Hirsch, *Social Limits to Growth* (Routledge and Kegan Paul, 1977), p. 141

2. Irving Kristol, 'The Disaffection from Capitalism in Capitalism and Socialism', (Michael Novak) (ed.) (American Enterprise Institute for Public Policy Research, Washington DC, 1979), p. 27

3. E.J. Mishan, *The Economic Growth Debate* (George Allen & Unwin, London, 1977), p. 265

4. *The Long Debate on Poverty,* Institute of Economic Affairs, Readings 9, 1974

5. J.M. Keynes, The Economic Consequences of the Peace, 1919, London

6. D. Meadows and others, 'The Limits to Growth', a Report on the Club of Rome's Project on the Predicament of Mankind (Earth Island 1972)

7. Richard Easterlin, 'Does Money Buy Happiness?' *The Public Interest* (Winter 1973)

8. Tibor Scitovsky, *The Joyless Economy* (OUP Oxford, 1976)

9. E.J. Mishan, *The Costs of Economic Growth* (Penguin, London 1967)

10. E.J. Mishan, ibid., p. 9

11. Joseph A. Schumpeter, *Capitalism, Socialism and Democracy* (Harper and Row 1976)

12. T.K. Galbraith, *The New Industrial State* (New York 1968)

13. E.J. Mishan, *The Economic Growth Debate* (George Allen & Unwin, London, 1977)

14. Jacques Ellul, *The Technological Society* (Alfred A. Knopf, New York, 1964)

15. ibid.

16. Both men have written extensively but I would recommend H. Dooyeweerd *Roots of Western Culture* (Wedge Publishing Foundation, Toronto, 1979) and I. Kristol, *Two Cheers for Capitalism* (New York, Basic Books, 1958)

17. Milton and Rose Friedman, *Free to Choose* (Secker & Warburg 1980)

18. F.A. Hayek, *Law, Legislation and Liberty* Vols I-III (Routledge & Kegan Paul), 1973

19. Hayek, ibid., Vol I, p. 37

20. Hayek, ibid., Vol. II, p. 109

21. Hayek, ibid., Vol. II, p. 112

22. Hayek, ibid., Vol II, p. 117

23. A. Smith, *The Wealth of Nations,* Vol I, Methuen, London, 1961

24. Bernard Mandeville, *The Fable of the Bees* (Pelican Books, 1970) p. 67

25. Milton and Rose Friedman, *Free to Choose* (Secker & Warburg 1980)

26. Daniel Bell, 'The Cultural Contradictions of Capitalism', *The Public Interest,* No. 21, Fall 1970

Chapter 2
The Challenge of Marxism

1. J. Mignez Bonino, *Christians and Marxists* (Hodder & Stoughton, 1976)

2. Freidrich Engels, *Selected Works II* (1950), quoted R.N. Carew Hunt, *The Theory and Practice of Communism* (Pelican 1963), p. 64

3. Marx, *Civil War in France,* 1891. Quoted in Introduction.

4. Freidrich Engels, *Anti-Dühring,* 1877

5. Marx, *Capital,* Lawrence & Wishart, London 1970, p. 20

6. ibid, p. 234

7. ibid, p. 235

8. Alexander Solzhenitsyn, *Warning to the Western World,* The Bodley Head & BBC, 1976

9. Marx, *Communist Manifesto,* 1848

10. ibid.

11. ibid.

12. Lenin, *The State and Revolution,* 1917

13. ibid.

14. Marx, *The Holy Family,* 1845

15. Marx, *Religion,* p. 42

16. V. Gardavsky, *God is not yet dead,* Penguin, 1973, p. 157

17. R.N. Carew Hunt, The Theory and Practice of Communism, Pelican, 1963, p. 29

18. Robert C. Tucker, *Philosophy and Myth in Karl Marx,* Cambridge University Press, 1971, p. 22

19. *Cigaro,* Vol. 19, 25 November 1978

20. 'Misconceptions About Russia are a Threat to America,' Alexander Solzhenitsyn, *Foreign Affairs,* Vol. 58, No. 4 (Spring 1980)

Chapter 3
Is Christianity Relevant?

1. R.H. Preston, *Religion and the Persistence of Marxism* (S.C.M. Press, London, 1979) p. 8

2. ibid., p. 8

3. G. Guttierrez, *A Theology of Liberation* (S.C.M. Press, London, 1974) p. 159

4. J. Mignez Bonino, *Revolutionary Theology Comes of Age* (SPCK, London, 1975) p. 88

5. R. de Vaux, *Ancient Israel* (Darton, Longman & Todd, London, 1976)

6. ibid.

7. Emil Brunner, *Justice and the Social Order* (Lutterworth Press, London and Redhill, 1946)

8. C. Hodge, *Systematic Theology* (Thomas Nelson & Sons, London and Edinburgh, 1874)

Chapter 4
Reforming the Market Economy

1. G.C. Allen, *The British Disease,* Hobart Paper 1967, (Institute of Economic Affairs, 1976)

2. M. Arnold, *Culture and Anarchy*

3. J.M. Keynes, 'My Early Beliefs'

4. A. Bryant, *English Sage (1840-1940)* (Collins with Eyre and Spottiswood, London, 1940) p. 215

5. H. Antonides, *Multinationals and the Peaceable Kingdom* (Clarke Irwin & Co. Ltd, Toronto 1978)

6. Charles Booth, *Life and Labour in London,* Macmillan & Co, 1889, p. 155

Chapter 5
Third World Poverty and First World Responsibility

1. Robert McNamara, *World Development Review* (International Bank for Reconstruction and Development, Washington, D.C., 1978)

2. Peter Townsend, *The Concept of Poverty* (Heinemann, London 1970) p. 41-2, quoted P. Bauer in *Equality, the Third World and Economic Delusion* (Weidenfeld and Nicholson, London, 1981) p. 67

3. Nicolae Ceausescu

4. S. Mooneyham, *What do You Say to a Hungry World?* Waco, Texas: Word Books, 1975, p. 128

5. J. Nyerere, 'The Economic Challenge: Dialogue on Corporation' *African Affairs* (April 1976)

6. R.J. Sider, *Rich Christians in An Age of Hunger,* Hodder & Stoughton, p. 141

7. Reuber et al, *Foreign Private Investment in Development* (OUP, Oxford, 1973)

8. *The Impact of Multinational Enterprises on Employment and Training* (ILO Geneva 1976)

9. W.B. Reddaway, *UK Direct Investment Overseas, Final Report* (Cambridge, 1968)

10. A. MacBean and V.N. Balasubramanyam, *A Positive Approach to the International Economic Order,* British-North American Committee, 1980

11. US Department of Commerce, *Survey of Current Business,* various issues

12. A. MacBean and V.N. Balasubramanyam, *A Positive Approach to the International Economic Order,* British-North American Committee, 1980.

13. *Transnational Corporations in World Development: A re-examination* (UN, New York 1978).

14. S. Watanabe, 'Exports and Employment, the case of the Republic of Korea', *International Labour Review* (December 1972)

15. R.L. Garner, International Finance Corporation 1961, Annual Meeting of Board of Governors, (September 1961)

16. E.F. Schumacher, *Small is Beautiful* (Abacus, London, 1974) p. 140

17. R.L. Garner, op. cit.

18. Max Weber, *The Religion of India,* the Free Press, New York, 1958 and *The Religion of China,* the Free Press, New York, 1951

19. A. Van Leeuven, *Christianity in World History,* (Edinburgh House Press, 1964)

20. *Harper's* (January 1970)

21. Independent Commission on International Development Issues, *North-South: a Programme for Survival* (Pan Books, London and Sydney, 1980)